HAUNTED
STEVENAGE

HAUNTED STEVENAGE

Paul Adams

The
History
Press

For Margaret Hughes

First published 2015

The History Press
The Mill, Brimscombe Port
Stroud, Gloucestershire, GL5 2QG
www.thehistorypress.co.uk

British Library Cataloguing in Publication Data.
A catalogue record for this book is available from the British Library.

ISBN 978 0 7509 5377 1

Typesetting and origination by The History Press
Printed in Great Britain

CONTENTS

ACKNOWLEDGEMENTS

BEFORE we begin exploring the haunted history of Stevenage I would like to take a moment to thank the following people who have helped in various ways with the research and writing of this book: my old friend Eddie Brazil, who has given his usual support and encouragement to the project as well as writing the foreword; the late Peter Underwood, for allowing me to use material and photographs from his unique archive on British ghosts and hauntings; Paul Bowes from Book Castle Publishing and author Ruth Stratton who helped with copyright issues and allowed me to quote from published sources; Richard Corbelli and Chris Body for taking the time to discuss their involvement with the case of the Stevenage Poltergeist; Damien O'Dell and Ashley Knibb, who provided material from the case files of the Anglia Paranormal Investigation Society (APIS); Clare Fleck, archivist at Knebworth House, who provided historical information as well as modern ghostly experiences; Des Turner, for allowing me to reproduce his article on 'The Ghost of Lady's Wood'; David Farrant, President of the British Psychic and Occult Society (BPOS), who revisited his investigation into the Minsden chapel haunting,

and Andrew Fazekas and Bill King of the Luton Paranormal Society (LPS) for access to their investigation reports on Minsden; John Hope, who invited me around haunted Little Wymondley Priory; Jo Clarke and Karen Quinn, who helped with collecting new material, as did Oliver Pritchard at the Stevenage *Comet*; Anya Ingarfill and Francesca Bartha for showing me around the much-haunted White Lion pub; and the staff at Stevenage Central Library who allowed access to their local studies collection. I would also like to thank all those Stevenage residents who spoke with me and allowed their original experiences to be included in this book. Where requested I have used pseudonyms but the identities of all those persons who described encounters with Stevenage's ghosts are known to me. I would also like to acknowledge Matilda Richards and Emily Locke at The History Press for seeing the project through to publication with their usual efficiency; and Bev Creagh of the *Luton News* for her continuing interest in my work. My children – Aban, Idris, Isa and Sakina – deserve yet another acknowledgement for their patience and inspiration; and finally Leah Mistry, who knows the reason why …

FOREWORD

GHOST – what an enigmatic word. For over 2,000 years ghosts have continued to baffle, puzzle and fascinate mankind. Yet in today's computer- and mobile phone-obsessed world the true nature of those things that go 'bump in the night' still evades scientific explanation. The *Oxford English Dictionary* defines the word *ghost* as the 'disembodied soul of a dead person haunting the living'. This description would conveniently fit most people's idea of the archetypal spook: a white-sheeted phantom which walks or glides the midnight corridors of a stately mansion or a romantic castle, moaning with clanking chains, completely unaware of being observed by the trembling spectator. However, years of research by paranormal investigators have revealed that there are many different types of what we would term a 'ghost'. They include poltergeists, crisis apparitions, 'stone tape' apparitions, atmospheric photographic ghosts, historical ghosts, and the curious enigma of phantasms of the living. All have their own peculiarities and ways of manifesting their presence or energy. If they all have one thing in common it is their rejection by established science as

amounting to proof of an afterlife, being looked upon as preternatural phenomena which will eventually be shown, by scientific means, to have a rational and logical explanation.

In 1882, a group of academics and eminent thinkers established the Society for Psychical Research (SPR) with the express purpose of scientifically investigating ghosts, haunted houses and the claims of mediums and psychics to be able to contact the dead. Over one hundred years on, even though our understanding of certain aspects of the paranormal have become clearer, the question still remains, *do ghosts exist and if so what are they?* Can mediums communicate with those who have passed on? Are poltergeists really spirit 'entities', or are the movements of objects and furniture in poltergeist hauntings the manifestation of externalised stress and frustration of adolescents? Is it places or people which are haunted, or is it, as many sceptics would have us believe, all nonsense?

It would appear that the quest and need for answers to a phenomenon which has mystified generations since the first account of a haunted house was described by Pliny the Younger in Greece twenty centuries ago still continues today. Throughout human history paranormal phenomena has been reported from almost every country on earth, by people of every race, creed and colour. Reports of hauntings and poltergeists regularly make the pages of the tabloids, yet despite years of research by dedicated investigators and the accumulation of mountains of compelling evidence, many people continue to scoff at the idea of ghosts. Quantative evidence is acceptable in the disciplines of medicine or physics; yet it does not seem to be satisfactory to many people in regard to the subject of ghosts. Perhaps there is a reason for this.

Today most people's perception and idea of ghosts stems from the reaction of the late eighteenth and early nineteenth-century Romantics against the advances made in science and the Age of Rationalism. The Romantics' response against forward-thinking philosophies, unleashed firstly by the Renaissance and the Reformation, and subsequently by ideas and values which were fuelled by advances in knowledge, was to retreat into the world of the imagination. Education and technology had freed Man's mind from the tyranny of ignorance, but spiritually had left him with nowhere to go. Rationalism had robbed him of his mystical safe haven, and the needs of a changing world cast him into an industrial hell hole from which the only escape was the mind. As a rebuff to the cold hard reality of science, the writers of the period – such as Horace Walpole, William Beckford, Mathew Lewis and Ann Radcliff – populated their Gothic novels with ghosts, monsters and fantastical creatures which

lurked and roamed within ruined abbeys, labyrinthine castles, dripping dungeons and moonlit graveyards. Supernatural fiction was the antidote to the banality of everyday existence and the fear that science would destroy Man's need for the supernatural. But, of course, the fictional ghost and those things which genuinely do go 'bump in the night' are two completely different things.

Ironically, 200 years on from the Romantics' hatred of science and rejection of the Age of Reason, modern-day scientists have moved that bit closer to establishing that ghosts, far from being romantic delusions or 'all in the mind' may well represent evidence of the survival of the human personality, albeit in the form of a psychic recording. If there is any truth to the 'stone tape' theory – that physical surroundings can absorb an impression of violent or tragic events and later, under a combination of circumstances or conditions and with the right person present, play back these recordings – one would certainly expect it to apply to many of the paranormal accounts contained in this book. For here the reader will encounter headless ghosts, phantom monks, violent poltergeists, spectral hounds, as well as invisible entities and ghostly children. Some may well be stone tape apparitions; others possibly historical photographic ghosts, atmospheric phantoms or elemental spirits. In some cases the incidents may well be a case of an overactive imagination. Only research and study will eventually help us understand the enigma of ghosts and reveal their true nature, for paranormal investigation is a journey of discovery and I can think of no one better qualified to guide the reader on an exploration of haunted Stevenage than the author of this book, paranormal historian, Paul Adams. I have known Paul for over ten years since we first met at Borley in Essex in September 2003 and to date we have co-authored three books on paranormal subjects together.

I suspect the majority of the readers of this book will have no trouble in accepting that the strange and curious incidents and accounts contained within represent genuine paranormal phenomena. There will also be those readers who, with open minds and an enquiring curiosity, will want to know more about the subject, as well as the sceptics who with wry smiles may chance to browse its pages. To all these readers I recommend that you draw the curtains, turn down the lights, check under the bed or behind the sofa, and let Paul Adams introduce you to the spooks, phantoms and ghosts of *Haunted Stevenage*.

Eddie Brazil
High Wycombe, Buckinghamshire
2015

INTRODUCTION

THIS is the first book devoted entirely to the ghosts and hauntings of Stevenage. Stevenage has featured in a number of other previous volumes by various authors concerned with the subject of the paranormal in the County of Hertfordshire but none have interested themselves completely with the accounts of strange and inexplicable happenings – both historic and modern – that have been recorded here over the course of many years. When I was asked to write this book I quickly realised that here was an opportunity to explore an aspect of the paranormal that has interested me personally for a long time, namely that ghosts can appear not only to the inhabitants of traditional locations such as old houses and stately homes, but also to ordinary people in modern dwellings and settings that have no previous history of hauntings or similar phenomena.

Today there has been an enormous surge of interest in the subject of the paranormal, fuelled over the past decade by the popularity of a number of reality television programmes on terrestrial as well as satellite and cable TV. The first of these, *Most Haunted*, which first aired in May 2002 and initially survived fourteen series over eight years, including several sensational live specials and spin-off programmes, brought the subject of ghost hunting and paranormal investigation to the attention of many ordinary people for the first time. However, despite the popularisation, what remains clear is that many people from all walks of life claim to have had paranormal experiences, often those who have no particular or continuing interest in the subject, the most common and familiar of these being encounters with ghosts and apparitions.

In his foreword, Ed Brazil has touched on some of the categories of ghost and hauntings that over time have become generally accepted by investigators as forming a framework into which many paranormal experiences seem to fall. One of these, the so-called 'stone tape', seems to explain why some apparitions appear to behave as though they are some kind of paranormal replay of past events that have somehow become imprinted on their surroundings and can, in the presence of a certain percentage of the population – those with some kind of psychic gift or insight – be seen and

The Old Town High Street, Stevenage. (Paul Adams)

experienced again. This kind of haunting is most often associated with buildings or structures of great age, where the cumulative emotions and events of a particular location seem to build up over time.

Stevenage, for the superficial visitor a modern 'new town', has a long and enviable connection with significant events in the evolving history of this country. And history and ghosts are in many ways one and the same thing. This goes back to Roman times with the town's strategic position within a day's march of the three most important centres created by the occupying Roman forces: Londinium (London), Verulamium (present-day St Albans), and Camulodunum (Colchester). The Romans' vast north–south highway from the Cripplegate fort in the south passed through the area we now know as Stevenage, joining another Roman road which ran from Verulamium in the south to present-day Baldock. In later times, a Saxon village was established

where the church of St Nicholas stands today whose name (derived as has been suggested by historians from the generic phrase 'At the strong oak' or 'strong gate') was eventually stabilised between the fourteenth and sixteenth centuries as 'Stivenhatch' and later 'Stivenach'. The prosperity that Stevenage achieved during the days of stagecoach travel along the Great North Road is evident in the many surviving inns and notable buildings that line the beautiful old High Street. In 1946, Stevenage's designation as a 'New Town' under the County of London Plan drawn up by the then Attlee Government, inaugurated a new era of the town's history. All of these events have in some way affected the psychic fabric of the region and result in the stories and encounters that you are about to read – researched either from existing records and accounts, or personally told to me by the people who experienced them and published for the first time.

Some of Stevenage's haunted places are well known to ghost hunters and aficionados of the supernatural. I have visited the delightful Minsden chapel on many occasions and its closeness to the town made it one location that without question deserved to be included. Also Knebworth House has a unique connection and association with the history of the paranormal that would have been conspicuous by its absence, while the coffin of Henry Trigg and its associated ghost stories have made it the town's most familiar and immediate icon of the macabre. However, the New Town hauntings are the ones that have interested me the most and prove that wherever you are, the world of the unseen is always close at hand.

No regional ghost book can ever claim to be complete. As old hauntings fade away, new ghosts are constantly being seen, convincing cases of haunting are always occurring and previously unreported accounts of supernormal activity gradually come into the public domain. I hope that this book will encourage this tradition of reporting to continue. I am always interested in collecting details of new experiences or learning further information on any of the cases and hauntings included in this book, either

The Queensway Clock Tower, commemorating the completion of the first phase of the New Town development in 1959. (Paul Adams)

for a future edition or a sequel volume – readers are welcome to contact me in confidence through my website.

It only leaves me to say that I hope you enjoy this book as much as I have researching and writing it.

Paul Adams
Luton, Bedfordshire
2015

1

THE LONELY GHOSTS OF MINSDEN

The History of a Ruin

Just under 2½ miles west of Stevenage town centre, close to the old B656 London Road, lies one of Hertfordshire's most enigmatic haunted sites, the lonely chapel of St Nicholas, a flint and rubble ruin now in an advanced state of decay. According to most accounts, Minsden chapel was built sometime in the early fourteenth century but fell into disuse around 1675, although marriages were

Minsden chapel, drawn by an unnamed artist in the Victorian era. The building has been a ruin for many years. (Peter Underwood Collection/Paul Adams)

occasionally held there for a further sixty years after that date. In 1690, the lead roof was stripped by thieves and the three chapel bells were also stolen in 1725. The last recorded wedding took place on 11 July 1738 when Enoch West and Mary Horn exchanged their vows in the now roofless building. It was on this occasion that a piece of falling masonry knocked the prayer book from the parson's hand, after which the Bishop of Lincoln closed the chapel for good, consigning Minsden to decades of neglect and decay. Today only the heavily eroded outer walls remain, hidden amongst trees on the edge of neighbouring farmland.

Minsden has enjoyed a haunted reputation stretching back many years but when this actually first became established is unclear. In the early 1900s a local photographer, T.W. Latchmore, visited the ruins and succeeded in capturing the figure of a hooded and sheeted apparition framed in one of the crumbling archways. Now something of an iconic image, this 'ghost' photograph is an undoubted fake and has done much to perpetuate the legend of a ghostly monk at Minsden over the years. According to the late Tony Broughall in his book *Two Haunted Counties* (2010), the appearance of the ghostly monk is heralded by the tolling of the stolen bells of Minsden. 'As the sounds fade away,' Broughall notes, 'the apparition of the monk appears beneath the arch on the south side of the ruins. Walking with head bowed in reverence, the figure enters the chapel's roofless shell and proceeds to climb invisible stairs to a long-since vanished bell tower where he disappears. A few minutes later, the sounds of beautiful yet wistful music is briefly heard before all is silent again.'

The famous Minsden chapel 'ghost', photographed by T.W. Latchmore in the early 1900s. (Author's collection)

As well as its phantom nun, there is a tradition that an early benefactor, known as Dame Margerie, who lived near Minsden in the 1300s, returns to the chapel from time to time, while the apparition of a small boy playing a flute is said to have been seen playing near the chapel by a visitor in the mid-1980s. There are also unsubstantiated stories connecting the site to the murder of a local nun and the existence of a lost tunnel running under and away from the ruins. Despite these colourful evocations, many visitors to the ruins claim to have experienced strange happenings and a number of psychic investigators have reported instances of alleged phenomena to the point that it would be unwise to simply dismiss the Minsden ghosts out of hand.

Early Investigations and Phenomena

In the late 1940s, Peter Underwood (1923–2014), the future President of the Ghost Club, then a young and upcoming paranormal researcher, conducted an all-night vigil at Minsden on All Hallows' Eve in the company of two equally enthusiastic local ghost hunters, Tom Brown, from nearby Weston and Derek Clark from Underwood's home town of Letchworth. A few days before, in preparation for their investigation, Underwood together with his brother John and accompanied by Tom Brown, had visited the ruins in daylight. On this occasion both Peter Underwood and Tom Brown heard what they were convinced was a distinct snatch of 'strangely fascinating' music; John Underwood, two steps behind his brother, heard nothing. There were no other visitors and the

Two rare photographs from the Peter Underwood investigation of Minsden in the late 1940s. John Underwood examines the chapel ruins and (above) Peter Underwood points out the spot where a luminous cross appeared on the stonework during a vigil held on 31 October 1947. (Peter Underwood Collection/Paul Adams)

chapel's remote location makes it unlikely that the sounds came from a nearby house or passing car. On 31 October 1947, the ghost hunters returned to the lonely Minsden chapel. During the course of their vigil a strange incident took place, as Underwood's original notes, reproduced here for the first time, describe:

Arrived 11.45.

Circled ruins looking for possible tramps, poachers etc.

Entered ruins & watched closely as 'the witching hour' passed. Continued wandering round ruins until 1.0am (Summer Time was in operation) when we hoped to witness some phenomena.

Nothing happened at 1.0am and we continued quietly walking round ruins until 1.45 when I saw a white cross which seemed to glow with unnatural brightness for a few seconds, then faded, only to reappear a few seconds later. It continued fading & reappearing for several minutes.

Both Mr Clark and Mr Brown saw the cross as well as myself.

It was a 'crux decussata' or Latin Cross and appeared on what had originally been part of the walls of the chapel.

It could possibly have been some trick of the moonlight, as a full moon was shining down on the ruins through the trees, though had it been anything to do with the branches one would have thought the cross would have been black and white.

The investigators eventually left the ruins at 2.45 a.m. 'Never have I felt so certain that a place was haunted as I stood among those silent crumbling ruins,' Underwood noted in an article written for the paranormal-themed *World Service*

journal in March 1949. 'A doorway at the east end I found much colder than the rest of the ruins.' Peter Underwood also included an account of his Minsden ghost hunt in his autobiography *No Common Task* published in 1983 in which he states that all three men were aware of an invisible presence that was sensed on several occasions beneath one of the ruined stone arches.

The Occult Connection

Another noted investigator with personal experience of Minsden chapel is David Farrant, president of the long-established British Psychic and Occult Society (BPOS), who is well known for his involvement in the Highgate Vampire media phenomenon of the early 1970s. In August 1983 during a daytime visit to the ruins, Farrant discovered evidence of an occult ceremony having taken place, a fate that has befallen a number of similar abandoned churches across the region, including Thundridge Old Church near Ware and most famously the old church of St Mary's at Clophill in Bedfordshire, subject of a recent film, *Paranormal Diaries: Clophill* (2013) by Hertfordshire-based filmmaker Kevin Gates.

In his book *Dark Journey* (2004), a collection of reports drawn from the files of the BPOS, David Farrant describes two historic experiences of strange happenings at Minsden chapel. On a warm summer afternoon in 1959, Peter Rosewarne from Baldock visited the chapel accompanied by a lady friend and his fox terrier dog. After spending some time in the ruins, the couple noticed that despite it being a sunny cloudless day, the interior of the chapel had

Psychic investigator David Farrant at Minsden in 1983. (BPOS)

become enveloped in a strange darkness which seemed completely unnatural. At the same time Rosewarne's dog became highly distressed and lay down whining and cringing on the ground. In 1975, again on a hot summer day, Mary Prowse from nearby Hitchin also experienced an unpleasant atmosphere at Minsden and obtained a colour photograph (subsequently examined by David Farrant) which seemed to show a cowled monk-like figure standing in the arched chapel entrance.

The Legacy of Reginald Hine

One person who was clearly affected by the stillness and atmosphere of Minsden chapel more than anyone else was the troubled Reginald Hine, a solicitor and writer whose two-volume history of his home town of Hitchin was said

Reginald Hine (1883–1949), who vowed to haunt Minsden, a place he loved in life, from beyond the grave. (Author's collection)

17

A memorial to Reginald Hine at the entrance to Minsden chapel. Hine's ashes were interred in a cairn inside the chapel ruins. (Paul Adams)

to have been compiled by candlelight in order to imbue its writing with a sense of the past. Born in 1883, Hine leased the ruins from the Church authorities for the duration of his life and spent many hours there, finding much-needed solace from a harsh and materialistic world which he ultimately found too much to bear. It was here, on All Hallows' Eve 1943, that he completed his autobiography, *Confessions of an Un-Common Attorney*, published in 1945, four years before his death. On 14 April 1949, Hine calmly walked off the platform at Hitchin railway station into the path of a London-bound locomotive and was killed instantly. As a young man he claimed to have had a vivid dream in which he took his own life.

Hine's ashes were interred appropriately at Minsden in a small clearing formed inside the ruins and circled with clumps of planted polyanthus and a low wall made from fallen stones. Later a stone slab was erected as a lasting monument which can be seen today amongst the undergrowth close to the north side of the chapel; a place he vowed to haunt from beyond the grave. In the second volume of his *History of Hitchin*, he noted solemnly, 'trespassers and sacrilegious persons take warning, for I will proceed against them with the utmost rigour of the law, and, after my death, and burial, I will endeavour, in all ghostly ways, to protect and haunt its hallowed walls'. The legacy of Reginald Hine hangs heavily over Minsden's broken and derelict shell and there are those who feel that in some way he has kept his promise to return and make his presence felt to both ghost hunters and the general public at large.

Modern Researchers and Strange Happenings

The tragic story of Reginald Hine, together with tales of ghostly monks and other happenings, continues to draw many visitors with an interest in the paranormal to Minsden's remote and isolated ruin. The extraordinary success of the *Most Haunted* television reality show has encouraged many people to form investigative groups of their own – in 2005, when amateur research into the paranormal was experiencing unprecedented levels of popularity in Britain, parapsychologist Dr Ciarán O'Keeffe, a frequent *Most Haunted* investigator, estimated that 750 separate paranormal societies were active in the country at any one time involving several thousand lay researchers and investigators.

Formed in 2003, the Luton Paranormal Society has carried out dozens of investigative vigils and ghost hunts across reputedly haunted sites in the three counties of Beds, Bucks and Herts, including three visits to the Minsden ruins, the first of which took place on 28 November 2003. On 17 April 2009, four society members, including President Andrew Fazekas and historian Bill King, returned to Minsden to hold a lengthy vigil and investigation. During the course of their visit, all members of the group reported experiencing unusual happenings including the sound of voices, touches as if from unseen hands and the impression of a black shadowy figure. They also witnessed several light anomalies, including strange blue flashes on the chapel stonework and in tree branches close to the ruined walls which the group were convinced were not caused by either their own equipment or, due to the isolated location, passing cars or other visitors. The Luton-based ghost hunters returned to Minsden for a third vigil on 9 September 2011. On this occasion seven members spent several hours in and around the ruins and were rewarded for their efforts by a number of unusual incidents. A few minutes before midnight, Bill King reported seeing a strange light shaped like a peanut shining on the ground when it was clear that none of the team were using their torches; breathing sounds, footsteps together with unusual smells were also reported. The group also spent some time experimenting with a version of the 'Ghost Box', a modified AM/FM radio set popular with some researchers, which has been suggested can pick up anomalous sounds and voices from discarnate spirits and similar 'entities'.

Clearly there is much scope for continued investigation here and Minsden chapel remains a unique and intriguing site that all those interested in the history of the paranormal should visit at some time.

Minsden chapel, on the outskirts of Stevenage. The ruins as they are today. (Paul Adams)

2

THE YELLOW BOY OF KNEBWORTH AND OTHER SPECTRES

Paranormal Connections

British ghostlore includes many accounts of prophetic hauntings involving super-natural omens of death and misfortune. Many are family or hereditary ghosts linked with a particular lineage or household, often involving members of the aristocracy. The banshee (from the Gaelic *bean si* or 'fairy woman') is a well-known death omen from Celtic folklore, an invisible screaming ghost reported from Ireland and the Western Highlands of Scotland whose mournful wailing is the announcement of an impending death in the family over which it acts as an unseen guardian and foreteller of sorrow. A specific example from Scotland is the phantom drummer boy or 'drum of death' associated with the ancient Airlie family and their family seat at Cortachy Castle in Kirriemuir, Angus. Apparitions or similar visible ghosts are also associated with prophetic hauntings, the most notable being the appearance of a glowing male figure or shining child known as the 'Radiant Boy'. Corby Castle in Cumbria has one of the most famous 'Radiant Boys', which appeared to the rector of Greystoke in 1803 and again to another visitor in 1834. Although not encountered now for many years, this haunting provides a neat introduction to the haunted history of Knebworth House, which lies close to the A1(M) dual-carriageway, 2 miles south of Stevenage town centre.

Knebworth and its History

Known today for its annual Sonisphere heavy-metal music festival and similar large-scale outdoor events, Knebworth has been the family seat of the Lytton family since the last years of the fifteenth century and provides Stevenage with a unique connection with the worlds of Victorian Spiritualism and British supernatural literature. Knebworth (from Chenepeworde or 'the house on the hill') is listed in the Domesday Book

Beautiful Knebworth House, one of Stevenage's most haunted buildings. (www.knebworthhouse.com)

of 1086 where a small fortified manor house, originally given to one of William the Conqueror's stewards, existed for a period of around 400 years surrounded by acres of rolling wood and parkland. In 1490, Sir Robert Lytton tore down what remained of the original manor house and erected a new Tudor building in the characteristic red 2in bricks of the time, built around a central courtyard. This building survived until the early 1800s when three of its four wings were demolished and the remaining (west) wing underwent extensive remodelling.

The Knebworth House that visitors see today, with its crenulated battlements, copper-clad cupolas and leering gargoyles, dates principally from 1843–45 when the novelist Edward Bulwer-Lytton, subsequently the 1st Baron Lytton, carried out another raft of renovation following the death of his mother, moulding Knebworth into the then increasingly fashionable Gothic Revival style. Further alterations were affected by the famous architect, Sir Edwin Lutyens. Today, Knebworth is the home of Henry Lytton-Cobbold and his family, Edward Bulwer-Lytton's great-great-great-grandson. The house's vivid appearance has made it a suitable location for a number of film and television productions. Horror fans will recall it as the home of the whistling Shadmock in Amicus' 1981 film *The Monster Club*, based on the stories of English writer R. Chetwynd-Hayes, while in 1988 Ken Russell filmed exterior scenes for his *The Lair of the White Worm*, an adaptation of *Dracula* author Bram Stoker's novel of the same name.

The Mystery of the 'Yellow Boy'

Knebworth boasts two interesting historical ghosts, the eerie-sounding 'Yellow Boy' and a musical haunting involving the unquiet spirit of a young girl known as 'Spinning Jenny'. The 'Yellow Boy' is a radiant phantom said to watch over the Lytton family and to appear as an omen of impending and violent death. The origins and evidence for the haunting are somewhat obscure and unsatisfactory, particularly as the most often cited account of its appearance appears not to have taken place in the way several writers have suggested. Robert Stewart, 2nd Marquess of Londonderry, known as Lord Castlereagh, Secretary of State for War in William Pitt the Younger's Government, the man who fought a duel with then Foreign Secretary and future Prime Minister George Canning on Putney Heath on 21 September 1809, is credited as having seen the ghost while staying a night in Knebworth's haunted room. In the morning, Stewart claimed to have seen the figure of a young boy with yellow hair which appeared from out of the fireplace and drew its fingers across its throat several times before disappearing. Unfortunately for Robert Stewart, the 'Yellow Boy' was to prove an omen of his own demise as on 12 August 1822 he committed suicide aged 53 by slashing his own throat with a penknife at his home at Loring Hall in Kent.

Although the location of Stewart's death is a matter of certainty, that of his alleged supernatural experience is not quite as clear cut. In his book *Irish Literary and Musical Studies*, published in 1914, Alfred Percival Graves, discussing the poetry of William Allingham

(1824–1899), suggests that the experience actually took place in a former barracks at Ballyshannon in County Donegal and that this is the ghost that John Gibson Lockhart describes in his biography of Sir Walter Scott – Stewart, at the urging of the Duke of Wellington, is said to have recounted his experience to Scott and Allingham subsequently immortalised the whole affair in his poem, 'The Goblin Child of Belashanny':

… When suddenly – Heaven! – the fire
Leaped up into a dazzling pyre,
And boldly from the brightened hearth
A Naked Child stepped forth.

With a total, frozen start,
A bound, – a pausing of the heart.
He saw. It came across the floor.
Its size increasing more and more
At every stride, until a dread
Gigantic form stood by his bed.

Glaring for some seconds' space
Down into his rigid face –
Back it drew, with steadfast look,
Dwindling every step it took,
Till the Naked Child returned
To the fire, which brightly burn'd
To greet it: then black sudden gloom
Sunk upon the silent room …

How the story of Lord Castlereagh's ghostly experience became transferred to Knebworth is today somewhat unclear as it appears to come from external written sources rather than being an oral tradition within the Lytton family. A prime candidate is a semi-autobiographical work, *Memories of Ninety Years* (1924), written by the Victorian painter Mrs Henrietta Ward and published the year of her death at Slough at the age of 92.

In a chapter entitled 'Recollections of Lord Lytton and Knebworth', Mrs Ward – who together with her husband was a guest at the house on a number of occasions – claims to have been told the story by Edward Bulwer-Lytton (see p.25) and that he suggested it took place during his father's lifetime. William Earle Bulwer died when his son was 4 years old, which dates the incident (if it occurred at all) to 1807 at the latest. How accurate Mrs Ward's memoirs are is open to debate, particularly as she notes that her husband was also told of another Lytton family ghost, a traditional death coach, which was heard to draw up to the front door of Knebworth House shortly before the death of a member of the household. There are a number of these particular hauntings associated with buildings and places around the country, such as at Acton Place near Long Melford in Suffolk where a coach steered by a headless driver careers along the country lanes and vanishes through the gates of the ruined house, at one time the home of the eccentric William Jennens (1701–1798), known as 'William the Miser', one of the richest men in eighteenth-century England who chose to live a great portion of his life in a basement room dressed in rags. The death coach has its strongest associations in Irish folklore where it is known as the Cóiste Bodhar or 'silent coach'.

The Tale of 'Spinning Jenny'

Harry Price (1881–1948), famous for his investigation of Borley Rectory, known to legions of paranormalists as 'the most haunted house in England', was one psychic investigator who became interested in the ghostly stories connected with Knebworth House. While researching for his *Poltergeist Over England* (1945), Price corresponded with the then Lord Lytton and found that the story of 'Spinning Jenny', or at least phenomena which was later described under that name, was an ancient one and was mentioned in some of the old records connected with the property. The haunting was connected with a particular room in the old Tudor east wing of the house. Here it is said that a young girl was kept in forced labour, spinning on a wheel for hours and days at a time. Half-starved and beaten, the unfortunate Jenny gradually went insane and, according to variations of the story, either committed suicide or was eventually found dead from malnutrition. After her death, the sound of her ghostly spinning wheel could be heard coming from inside her former prison, accompanied by the poltergeist-like movement of objects. When the east wing was demolished along with several other parts of the original Tudor house (Price gives a date of 1811 for these alterations), the ghost of 'Spinning Jenny' was heard no more.

As with many haunted houses across the country, colourful stories often come into being as a means of both explaining the supposed mechanics of reported ghost sightings and similar strange happenings as well as putting them within a human frame of activity. The ghost of 'Spinning Jenny' at Knebworth is a case in point. Harry Price was able to examine a reprint of a rare and privately printed pamphlet, *The History of Jenny Spinner, the Ghost of Knebworth House [Written by Herself]* which was originally published in London in 1800 when the haunted room was still in existence. It was composed

her ending is a happy one as she is rescued from her prison and her sinister captor ultimately gets his just desserts. Although the whole story of 'Spinning Jenny' is clearly fictional, it seems highly likely that at some point in Knebworth's past, paranormal phenomena (aural and possibly physical – Price suspected a poltergeist 'infestation') that gave the impression of the operation of a spinning wheel were experienced in the former Tudor east wing over time and which today survives in a colourful romance which itself is now over 200 years old.

Stories from the Séance Room

Knebworth's most high-profile owner was the nineteenth-century novelist Edward Bulwer-Lytton (1803–1873), author of *Godolphin* (1833) and *The Last Days of Pompeii* (1834), whose tales of the supernatural were highly regarded in their day. In 1859, *Blackwood's Magazine* published his novella *The Haunted and the Haunters* which describes a fictional ghost hunt in a house in London, home of the sinister 'Shadow'. The story may have been influenced by the famous 'electric horror' of No.50 Berkeley Square which became known as the most haunted house in London during the first half of the nineteenth century (see my *Extreme Hauntings* (2013), pp.15-21, for a concise account of the case). Another possible source of inspiration, certainly where the ghostly effects recorded in Bulwer-Lytton's story are concerned, is his friendship with Daniel Dunglas (D.D.) Home (1833–1886), (pronounced 'Hume'), regarded as one of the most powerful mediums of the period.

Ghost hunter extraordinaire Harry Price (1881–1948), famous for his investigation of Borley Rectory, who investigated the hauntings of Knebworth House in the 1940s. (Stewart P. Evans)

at Christmastime of that year by a Miss E.M. James, then aged 25, who during a party at Knebworth House responded to a challenge to the guests to write an account of the origins of the spinning ghost, in much the same way that Mary Shelley created *Frankenstein* and John Polidori set down his *The Vampyre* (a seminal story from which it is possible to trace the origins of Stoker's *Dracula*) at the Villa Diodati on the shore of Lake Geneva in 1816. Miss James' account was completed in three days and for inspiration drew on the traditional theme of a starved spinning girl which was commonplace in the house at the time. Fortunately for Jenny

Today we are familiar with mental mediums such as Colin Fry, Derek Acorah and Sally Morgan. These mediums give public demonstrations and private readings involving clairvoyance and other psychic abilities which are only experienced by the mediums themselves, who pass on alleged information received to the sitters. Home was what is known as a physical medium whose phenomena involved the production of physical effects such as the movement of objects and in rare cases the production of materialisations of alleged spirit forms. During his lifetime, Home achieved international celebrity status and gave séances to wealthy patrons across Europe, including crowned rulers and members of the aristocracy. Never caught in fraud, his reputation today remains high, which may be something of a surprise given the astonishing

The nineteenth-century novelist Edward Bulwer-Lytton (1803–1873), at one time the owner of Knebworth House, whose interests included both fictional and real ghost stories. (www.knebworthhouse.com)

happenings said to have taken place in his presence, which read like something out of a fairy story. As well as making an accordion move and play tunes on its own, Home's phenomena also included the appearance of apparitions and spirit hands, the movement of objects and furniture, eerie footsteps, as well as the startling elongation of the medium himself, who also rose unaided into the air and handled burning coals from the fire grate without injury. Probably the greatest of these paranormal feats is his famous levitation and flight through two open windows three floors above street level at Ashley House in London (now demolished), said to have taken place on the evening of Sunday, 13 December 1868 which was witnessed collectively by three people, including Lord Adare and Lord Lindsay.

In the mid-1850s, Home gave séances for Edward Bulwer-Lytton at his London house in Park Lane and was later invited to Knebworth where he was received on several occasions over a period of ten years. Despite being impressed by Home's abilities – he wrote the medium a testimonial acknowledging 'the extraordinary phenomena which are elicited by your powers' – Bulwer-Lytton did not believe that spirits or discarnate souls of the dead had anything to do with the wonders he and the other sitters who fell under the medium's sway experienced. Rather they were 'certain physical idiosyncrasies which no study can acquire' or supernormal faculties of the human organism, and as such Bulwer-Lytton never became a convinced Spiritualist. For a writer, Home was too good a personality not to make use of and Bulwer-Lytton incorporated some of the great medium's characteristics in the character of Margrave, the sorcerer-hero of his 1862 novel, *A Strange Story*.

Edward Bulwar-Lytton's other connection with the world of Victorian Spiritualism concerns his association with James Manby Gully (1808–1883), a physician who practiced as a hydrotherapist and homeopathic doctor at his clinic in Malvern, Worcestershire. Bulwer-Lytton visited Gully in the hope of curing various ailments and stayed for over two months. Gully's treatment involved a vigorous regime of cold baths (often the patients were wrapped in wet blankets and had buckets of cold water thrown over them), plain food and physical exercise. James Gully was a convinced Spiritualist and later became President of the Spiritualist Association of Great Britain. Like Bulwer-Lytton, he attended sittings with D.D. Home, but his most famous mediumistic association is that of Florence Cook (1856–1904), the London physical medium who gave experimental sittings for the noted chemist, Sir William Crookes (1832–1919). A famous photograph, taken by Thomas Harrison, editor of *The Spiritualist* newspaper, shows Dr Gully taking the pulse of an alleged materialised spirit named 'Katie King' who was a regular visitor to Miss Cook's (later Mrs Corner's) séances.

The Many Ghosts of Knebworth

Today, Knebworth House itself is a popular visitor and tourist attraction that hosts weddings, corporate functions and similar events. Ghosts and supernatural happenings continue to be a part of the history of the house and there are a number of modern encounters which have been recorded as taking place here with some regularity since the time that students were billeted at Knebworth during the Second World War. This was the occasion when a ghostly figure was seen emerging through a panelled door in the Hampden Bedroom, sat on the apartment's impressive four-poster bed and then disappeared through another door in the opposite wall. This particular ghost was thought to be the seventeenth-century Parliamentarian John Hampden (*c*.1595–1643) after whom the room is named.

The name Cobbold was introduced into the Lytton family in April 1930 when Lady Hermione Bulwer-Lytton married Cameron Cobbold (1904–1987), the 1st Baron Cobbold and a former Lord Chamberlain and Governor of the Bank of England. In recent years, Lady Cobbold and a number of other people have seen an apparition known as the White Lady which haunts the house's

The famous Victorian medium Daniel Dunglas Home (1833–1886) whose séances took place at Knebworth House. (Author's collection)

Picture Gallery. This particular ghost is said to appear in the form of a white shadow which moves seemingly unaware of any other presence in the room before vanishing away. A former estate employee, Jack White, reported an unusual experience in the Picture Gallery one day while winding several antique clocks kept in the room. This was a delicate job which Mr White always carried out with great care. As he turned the winding key in one of the timepieces he was poked firmly in the ribs by what seemed a solid hand. Assuming it was his wife Pam, he turned to tell her off and was astonished to find that he was completely alone in the room. At one time the Picture Gallery was said to contain a portrait whose expression clearly changed from time to time but details of this today are sadly lacking.

Another employee at the house has claimed to have had supernatural experiences in and around the house practically from the day she started work. Knebworth archivist Claire Fleck described to the present author the experiences of Patti, who was employed as a nanny to Lord Cobbold's children in the mid-1980s. On entering the park to be interviewed for the position, she passed a man with red hair and beard sawing wood in the garden of the North Lodge. On asking if he could direct her to the Cobbold residence, the man replied that there was no one of that name on the estate. Somewhat bemused, Patti continued on her way and was successfully employed by the family. The identity of the North Lodge gardener is something of a mystery as there was no one living on the estate or employed by

Knebworth House – the haunted Picture Gallery. (www.knebworthhouse.com)

Knebworth House – an historic photograph showing part of the grand interior. (Author's collection)

the Cobbolds at Knebworth at that time. An unconfirmed account suggests that Patti's description of the figure matches a former worker who hanged himself in the grounds many years ago. At Knebworth, Patti also described experiencing the sensation of a cat clawing at her and the bedclothes as she lay in bed in the house one night. In the morning she noticed old scratch marks on the door and at the time the Cobbolds did not possess a cat of any kind.

Several members of the Cobbold family have reported experiencing inexplicable footsteps on the staircases and along the corridors inside the house, as well as lights turning themselves on and off for no apparent reason. Two particularly haunted parts of Knebworth House are the Tower Room and a chamber which is known as Mrs Bulwer's Room, both used as bedrooms for visiting guests of the family. Here people have experienced unpleasant and powerful sensations – on one occasions a family friend awoke in the night with the terrifying feeling of having invisible hands around her neck as though an unseen person was attempting to strangle her. In contrast to this unnerving encounter, the ghost of Edward Bulwer-Lytton is said to haunt his former study and drawing room, a gentle presence returning to the place he loved in life.

Another ghostly incident, experienced collectively by several people, took place during the daytime and involved a guided tour to members of the public given by one of Knebworth's regular house guides. After viewing the Banqueting Hall, the party passed through into the Dining Parlour, the last person being asked to close the door from the Hall behind them. As the guide resumed her talk, there were three sudden loud bangs on the door they had all just passed through. Assuming that the House Warden had allowed some late-comers on to the tour, the guide went and opened the door but there was no one in the immediate vicinity and the Warden was some distance away at the other end of the Hall. Closing the door, the talk resumed, only to be interrupted again by a further three loud raps on the same door. Again the tour guide opened the door and was somewhat alarmed to find the Banqueting Hall deserted. The whole process was repeated in total three times in front of a party of over a dozen people, one of whom commented: 'It's a ghost and it wants to join the tour.' The guide, who still works at Knebworth, could not explain the incident and it remains a mystery to this day.

One final ghost at Knebworth is not the sort of supernatural happening that would readily come to mind in connection with a haunted English country house. This is the alleged apparition of a phantom Second World War Churchill tank which lumbers slowly away from the Lodge gates in the direction of Codicote village, its turret hatch open and in which the figure of a steel-helmeted soldier is observed gesturing for those on the roadway to take cover, as if warning of an imminent German air raid. An account of this unusual haunting – a wartime equivalent of the traditional spectral coach and horses – was collected in the 1970s by Tony Broughall and presumably stems from the fact that Knebworth House was used as a transit station for British tanks in the early part of the war. How frequent the appearance of the ghostly tank has been in the past is now not readily known for sure.

3

SIX HILLS HAUNTINGS AND OTHER ANCIENT PLACES

The Hounds of Death

The Six Hills, Stevenage's most familiar landmark, have existed in their present form for centuries. Created around AD 100, these strange grass-covered mounds are barrows built by the occupying Roman forces for the burial of a wealthy and possibly land-owning local family. The hills themselves have changed little down through the years, although the surrounding area has undergone much alteration and development, particularly in the post-war period during the creation of Stevenage New Town and subsequent road alterations which have left the monuments remote and isolated. An original trackway parallel to the mounds, present in Roman times, eventually became the line of the Great North Road and the Six Hills were a familiar sight to travellers entering the town on foot and later by stagecoach from the south.

Not surprisingly given their strange appearance, colourful legends have grown up around the apparent origins of the Six Hills, the most well known of which is the story of the Devil who, to pass the time one day, hewed half-a-dozen clods of earth from nearby Whomerley Wood and threw them at innocent passers-by, thereby creating the bizarre line of grass-covered humps. According to this account, a seventh shot went astray and struck the tower of the village church of St Mary's at Graveley 2 miles north of the town. The mysterious nature of the monuments is reinforced in a number of conversations the present author has had with townsfolk during the researching and writing of the present book. In good horror story tradition, a modern legend has grown up of unexpected happenings and misfortune taking place to those who have rashly tried to dig into the mounds in search of buried treasure or similar artefacts. These include unnamed archaeologists and metal-detector enthusiasts who seem not to have lived to tell the tale! However, ancient earthworks and barrows, as well as the sites of former gallows and gibbets (often located at crossroads and the intersection of highways), are often associated with Black Dog or 'Black Shuck' hauntings, and this is the case with the Six Hills of Stevenage where the traditional appearance of a phantom hound has seemingly been reinforced by sightings that have apparently taken place as late as the 1960s.

In 1910, the Hertfordshire historian William Blythe Gerish (1864–1921) received a letter from a female correspondent that described two incidents of the appearance of a black dog apparition. One involved the lady herself, who claimed to have seen a large black hound as big as a donkey, which rose up out of the ground in front of her and a party of friends as they walked together along a path in Bury Mead to the north of the Old Town High Street. The second involved a local gamekeeper, who described seeing a large black dog which rushed past him in the darkness and disappeared in the direction of the Six Hills barrows. A short time later, as he approached Whomerley Wood to the north-east of Monks Wood (see p.35 onwards), he saw the same animal again which appeared behind him as though it were following his trail between the trees. Frightened, the unnamed gamekeeper (Gerish's correspondent also requested anonymity) abandoned his journey home and spent the night in the house of a nearby friend. As a gamekeeper familiar with various types of animal including hunting dogs, the appearance of the black hound was presumably strange and sinister enough for the countryman to believe he was seeing some kind of apparition.

The enigmatic Six Hills – Roman burial mounds said to be haunted by the apparition of a phantom black dog. (Paul Adams)

There are many derivatives of these traditional ghost dog hauntings and they go by a number of striking and colourful local names. The North of England is known as the hunting ground of 'Padfoot', an animal the size of a donkey whose feet are turned backwards; in Lancashire a similar beast is called by a number of names including 'Trash', 'Striker' and the 'Boggart' which when seen utters a terrible screeching sound before sinking down into the ground and disappearing. In Northumberland and parts of Yorkshire, the 'Barguest' is described as being a large black dog with blazing eyes, while 'Shuck' or 'Shag' haunts the cemeteries and graveyards of East Anglia on dark stormy nights, terrifying wayward travellers unlucky enough to cross its path with its single flaming eye. The legend of the 'Black Dog' phantom hound ghost is most strong in the West Country where it is known from a number of locations including Uplyme in Devon and the Blackmoor Gate crossroads on Exmoor. One phantom hound that breaks the tradition, however, is the Scottish 'Lamper' that haunts the wilds of the Hebrides Islands and whose appearance is considered to be an omen of approaching death. This ghostly dog is said to be white rather than the traditional black and to have no visible tail.

Mystery of the Bloodstained Man

With no recent accounts on record of the Six Hills Hound it may be that either this is a genuine haunting that has faded out over time, or a self-perpetuating local legend that has gradually lost its impetus in recent times. However, the Hills still have the power to mystify, as this account given to the present writer by a correspondent, Jaden Harris (pseudonym), clearly proves. Late one night in 2012, Jaden and her boyfriend were returning home after an evening out in Stevenage town centre. The couple live in a flat in Tippett Court off the B197 London Road close to the Six Hills, and as they drove south past the Asda supermarket the roadway and the curious grassed humps seemed to be deserted. Suddenly both Jaden and her partner were startled to see a figure which seemed to appear out of nowhere in the wide grass verge adjacent to one of the large domed mounds and move in a straight line out towards a point in the middle of the carriageway in front of their car. Fearing a collision, Jaden braked hard and the car passed close to the figure, which had reached the kerb and appeared to be about to step out into the road. Both saw a man in dark clothes whose face and hands – which were raised out in a gesturing manner in front of his body – appeared to be covered with blood.

Now terrified, Jaden accelerated away down the London Road and in her haste missed the left-turn into Tippett Court. A hundred yards further on she turned the car round and headed back up the road. By now the couple had calmed down and, suspecting the unidentified man had been involved in either a fight or an accident, decided to drive back and offer assistance. However, when they reached the spot where the figure had appeared the area around the barrows was completely deserted. Despite driving up and down the road several times and circling the car parks of the office buildings on the east side of the Six Hills, they could not find the mystery man. It seemed impossible for him to have moved away in the minute or so that it had taken to turn the car around and drive back past the mounds. The incident remains unexplained, although Jaden Harris is convinced that both she and her partner had encountered a ghost that night.

The Romans of Gunnel's Wood Road

Gunnel's Wood Road, running parallel with the A1(M) dual-carriageway, is named after a Scandinavian woman (Margaret Ashby in her *Stevenage: History & Guide* (2002), suggests a Dane from the time of the Viking raids) whose title survived into the fourteenth century as the name of an open area of playing field. In the mid-1950s a vast 65-acre industrial site was established by English Electric Aviation Ltd which after several mergers became British Aerospace, at one time Stevenage's single largest employer. There is a local tradition of a haunting by a marching column of Roman soldiers in the industrial area, stemming, so most accounts imply, from the levelling of a burial mound similar to those at the Six Hills which was removed in order to make way for the construction of new buildings. Like several 'stone tape' ghost reports, these Roman soldiers are said to appear floating at least 3ft above the surface of the ground, their position corresponding to the landscape they would have known in life. The story is an interesting one but whether there is any truth to the story or there have been modern manifestations is difficult to ascertain.

A recreation of the phantom Roman army, said to haunt the area around Gunnels Wood Road. (Eddie Brazil)

The Headless Ghost of Monks Wood

'For centuries man has been fascinated by tales of haunted houses: houses in which ghostly figures walk, eerie voices cry out, and in which furniture levitates in the air and floats to and fro. Many people don't believe that such things really exist. But they are wrong!' So stated American psychical researcher D. Scott Rogo in the introduction to his *The Haunted House Handbook* published in 1978. For the general public, the most obvious and familiar association with the world of the paranormal is through the concept of the haunted house, which in Britain alone must number in the tens of thousands, from ordinary flats and council houses through to large private dwellings, stately homes and castles. However, the annals of organised paranormal investigation easily reveal that ghostly activity takes place wherever there exists or has existed the presence of man, and the natural world, like the built environment, is a strange and haunted realm: there are haunted lakes, rivers, caves, hills, moorland and mountains, but perhaps after the haunted house, dark woods and forests are the next places where it would seem most natural for ghosts and phantoms to dwell.

Eerie Monks Wood – the ponds where a headless draped figure is said to walk. (Paul Adams)

There are many allegedly haunted woods across the country. Salcey Forest near Northampton is home to several unidentified phantom figures as well as the ghostly sounds of two fighting men, said to be a psychic echo of two long-dead prize-fighters; close to Fanton Hall at Basildon, Shrieking Boy Wood gets its name from a child murder carried out in the 1700s and the ghostly form of its tragic victim; while Clapham Wood, a few miles north-west of Worthing on the South Downs, came to prominence in the 1970s and early 1980s for a whole raft of strange and unsettling happenings including Black Magic rituals, unidentified shapes and figures, human disappearances, the levitation of witnesses as well as numerous UFO sightings.

Monks Wood lies on the southern side of Stevenage town centre; like the Six Hills just over half a mile to the north, it is an ancient site and was formerly part of the parish of Shephall. Local tradition, no doubt inspired by the name, suggests a monastery once stood on the site but this is not supported by the historical records. The Domesday Book of 1086 lists two manors in Shephall, both of which came under the lordship of St Albans church, and the woodland, most likely of oak and hornbeam, was used as grazing for pigs. Up until the Dissolution of the Monasteries by Henry VIII in the 1530s, the Manor of Shephall was administered by the Benedictine monks of St Albans. In 1542 it was given to the Nodes family and remained in their possession for nearly 300 years. In 1938, Monks Wood was bequeathed by its then owner, Mr Riches, to Gonville and Caius College, Cambridge, and in 1952 it was compulsorily purchased and replanted with conifers as part of the New Town by Stevenage

HEADLESS MONK IN THE NIGHT

EERIE tales are told about Monks Wood in Stevenage.

Supposedly the site of an ancient monastery, the frightening figure of a headless monk is said to return every six or seven years, floating over the pond deep in the heart of the wood.

Nonsense? One person who definitely believes the story is 11-year-old Kim Cook of Meadow Way, Stevenage.

One night last week, Kim says, he SAW the ghost, a faceless figure in a monk's habit and a ball-and-chain round its ankles, floating among the trees.

Kim ran away, and now, says his mother Joyce Cook, he won't go near the wood. "He's too scared to go over there," she said.

Kim's friend, Jackie Byfield, of Holly Copse, Bedwell, has seen the ghost, and so have lots of other people, according to Mrs Cook.

But when Kim's older brothers went ghost-hunting in the wood the same night all they saw was a spooky glow.

Stevenage police also investigated the area where

By MARTYN CORNELL

Kim says he saw the ghost, but could find nothing.

"There's no doubt the boy saw something," said a police spokesman. "But what he saw is another matter."

Stevenage Museum curator Mr Colin Dawes dismissed the idea that the apparition and the glow could be caused by marsh gas.

Mr Dawes said the story of the old monastery in the wood was almost certainly untrue.

"We believe the name Monks Wood was given when the land in and around Stevenage was owned by the Abbey of Westminster," he said, "and is nothing to do with any local monastery."

● Kim Cook (left) is pictured with his drawing of the 'ghost.' With him is friend Paul Pursehouse.

An article from the Stevenage Comet in 1974 covering an alleged sighting of the Monks Wood ghost. (Author's collection)

Development Corporation, today known as Stevenage Borough Council. It remains an atmospheric location with a *Blair Witch* quality, particular the area around the two ponds near its centre, and is popular with dog walkers.

With its name and religious associations – both real and imagined – it should be no surprise that any alleged haunting connected with Monks Wood has a decidedly monastic flavour. A draped black figure, said to be the cyclical apparition of a headless monk, has been rumoured to haunt the site for many years, returning to the ponds every six or seven years where it floats silently over the water. In 1974, 11-year-old Kim Cook from Meadow Way in Bedwell claimed to have seen the ghost one evening while out playing in Monks Wood on his own. An account of his encounter was published in the *Comet* newspaper in which he described seeing a faceless figure in a monk's habit (with a ball-and-chain round its ankles for good measure) floating amongst the trees. A schoolfriend, Jackie Byfield of Holly Copse, also claimed to have seen the ghost while Kim Cook's older brothers, who ventured into the wood the same night that their brother ran home to raise the alarm, told reporter Martyn Cornell that they had observed a 'spooky glow' amongst the trees. The young boy's experience was such that the local Stevenage police felt obliged to make an examination of the area but nothing untoward came to light at the time. 'There's no doubt the boy saw something,' a spokesman was quoted as saying, 'but what he saw is another matter.' Recurring or cyclical hauntings often wind down or become less powerful over time, with the result that the Monks Wood phantom may not be as active today as it was in the late 1960s/early 1970s.

A Spectre on Campus

The haunting of Monks Wood itself remains an intriguing mystery and there may be some connection with a neighbouring site to the north on the opposite side of the A602 Monkswood Way. In 2006, while working on a revised edition of their previously published book, *Haunted Hertfordshire* (2002), local researchers Ruth Stratton and Nicholas Connell collected an account of a ghostly figure seen haunting the corridors of the then recently constructed Stevenage campus building of the North Hertfordshire College. The apparition, described as having a monk-like appearance, was said to have been encountered on a number of occasions by the campus' ancillary staff, including a cleaner, site managers and security guards. The figure was mostly seen walking along an upper corridor as well as in a community hall on the ground floor and Stratton and Connell suggest that the phantom monk may have transferred its haunting from the old college premises opposite the Six Hills mounds (now occupied by the Asda supermarket), where caretaking staff are said to have experienced the poltergeist-like movement of objects and also appearances of a similarly monkish apparition before the former campus building was closed and demolished.

Ruth Stratton, who worked at the college between 2004 and 2006, was able to interview older members of staff who recalled a number of incidents including items being thrown around inside a storage shed on the old campus site as well as a number of sightings of a silent black-clad figure. To date there have been no reports of similar phenomena in or around the new supermarket

The modern Stevenage campus building of the North Hertfordshire College, where a monk-like figure has been seen walking the corridors. (Paul Adams)

building, the suggestion being that the haunting has somehow moved its focus to the recently constructed college building. The idea of a haunting moving in this way is not without precedent. In a famous case, the ghosts of Borley Rectory are thought by some researchers to have transferred their haunting to the twelfth-century church opposite following a fire and the subsequent demolition of the original rectory in 1944. Numerous accounts of strange and unusual happenings, including footsteps, mysterious smells and odours, the sound of the church organ being played (when the building was known to be unoccupied), together with sightings of a grey nun-like figure were recorded by the incumbent, the Revd Alfred Henning, along with numerous visitors throughout the late 1940s and through into the following decade. Alteration work, including physical changes and structural alterations, can also have an effect on the psychic fabric of a house or building: in some cases an existing haunting can lessen or cease entirely, or in others a new haunting can be created or somehow brought to life.

A Solitary Pikeman and Two Quarrelling Parsons

Mention of the Domesday village of Graveley just north of Stevenage earlier in this chapter brings to mind some supernatural associations which can be included in the present book at this point. In his *Two Haunted Counties* (2010), Tony Broughall suggests that a tradition of haunting associated with the English Civil War

(1642–1651) has been prevalent around Graveley for many years. There are several similar stories told across the county of Hertfordshire concerning Civil War ghosts: Berkhamsted Castle, the former Priory at Hitchin, Salisbury Hall near London Colney, and Watton-at-Stone village all have associations with both Royalist and Parliamentarian hauntings. Hertfordshire was very much Parliamentarian territory with its stronghold in the city of St Albans, and at Graveley the sounds and possibly apparitions of marching Roundhead soldiers are said to have been experienced with some frequency since those days. Broughall suggests that the phenomena had all but ceased towards the middle of the twentieth century although an account collected by Bill King of the Luton Paranormal Society suggests that occasionally it is possible to obtain a glimpse back into those violent and turbulent days.

To the north of Graveley the B197 road crosses a rise known as Jack's Hill and it was here at dusk one evening in 1982 that Daphne McCarthy had an unusual experience. As she drove along the road towards Graveley village she saw a man standing in a gap between the hedgerow on one side of the road. Immediately the figure's stance and appearance looked curiously out of place and in the few seconds between sighting him and drawing level in the car she was able to describe a soldier with a distinctly Roundhead appearance: the figure wore a visored helmet and breastplate and was holding what seemed to be a long wooden pole or pikestaff in its hands. The soldier had its eyes downcast towards the ground and appeared not to be aware of the car as it approached. Startled by what she had seen, Daphne

quickly glanced in the rear mirror but to her somewhat astonishment the gap between the hedges was empty and in a split-second the ghostly Roundhead had vanished.

In Graveley village itself there are ghostly associations with the Waggon and Horses pub, one of three former houses facing the High Street which date back to the eighteenth century or possibly earlier, although when I visited in the summer of 2014 the current owners claimed not to have experienced anything out of the ordinary.

One final story from the Graveley area concerns a plot of land known posthumously as Parson's Field, which during the 1300s was the setting for a violent and ultimately murderous quarrel. At this time the parson of Graveley, John Smyth, was involved in a long-standing feud with the incumbent of neighbouring Chesfield over the delineation of the boundary line running between the two parishes. Things came to a head in a sudden outburst which left the Chesfield parson, Robert Shorthale, lying dead in a field. John Smyth was found guilty of the crime but was eventually pardoned in 1384. Subsequently the site of the murder was said to be haunted by Parson Shorthale's ghost but details of any phenomena have become lost over time, as has the actual location of the crime. Around 1445, long after John Smyth was dead, the parishes of Graveley and Chesfield were combined and in 1750 the Bishop of Lincoln granted approval for the parish church at Chesfield to be demolished. St Mary's church at Graveley, the legendary target of the Devil's idle clod-throwing, remains the only reminder of this unusual rural tale.

The Mysterious Churchyard of St Nicholas

With their tilting tombs and ivy-covered monuments, often interspersed with dark and shadowy yew trees, long associated as a symbol of life and death and with the power to repel the forces of witchcraft and restrain the spirits of the dead, churchyards are easily the most atmospheric locations connected with tales of ghosts and hauntings, both by day and, more importantly, by night. A number of churches across Hertfordshire have ghostly associations, including the church of St Nicholas in Rectory Lane, Stevenage, whose reputation as the haunting ground of a phantom black hound seems to stretch back as far as the 1800s. Such a haunting is normally a variation of the 'Church Grim', a figure from both English and Scandinavian folklore said to act as a guardian spirit over the buried dead and normally considered to be the first person laid to rest in the churchyard. The Revd Sabine Baring-Gould (1834–1924), a churchman with a long interest in the supernatural and author of *The Book of Were-Wolves* (1865), suggested that one way to avoid a human spirit acting as the 'Grim' was to bury a black dog (entirely black without one white hair on its body) in the churchyard so that the dog's ghost would watch over the graves for eternity. Where St Nicholas' churchyard is concerned, local legend assigns this particular ghost as being that of a local dog poisoned to death by a church bell-ringer driven to distraction by its incessant barking, and for good measure two other ghosts said to make an occasional appearance are the solitary figure of a Roman legionnaire and the armour-clad apparition of St Nicholas himself mounted on a white horse.

St Nicholas' church, Stevenage – a ghost dog has long been reputed to haunt the churchyard. (Paul Adams)

Occupying the site of a small Saxon village, the original wooden church was replaced in the twelfth century and the stone tower with its characteristic Hertfordshire 'spike' (a fourteenth-century addition) is the only part of the building which remains from that time, the nave, aisles, chapels and vestry having been altered and rebuilt several times down through the centuries. Although modern reports of its ghost dog are non-existent, some mysterious aspect of former times does seem to survive at St Nicholas, as long-time Stevenage resident Alison Smith found out while walking through the churchyard with her dogs one winter's night in the 1980s. As she passed through the kissing gate and made her way along the pathway between the gravestones, she immediately became aware of a distinct change in the atmosphere and a strange bluish aura which seemed to both light up the surrounding grass and at the same time make the familiar outline of the church building indistinct, almost as though it were somehow fading from sight. Coming to a halt, Alison had the clear impression of several figures which came towards her out of the blue haze. Like moving shadows, the figures had no discernible features but appeared to stream past her, as though she were standing in the midst of a moving crowd. The experience lasted for around two minutes, after which the entire vision faded from sight and the normal aspect of the churchyard at night came back to life.

Interestingly throughout the entire episode, both dogs showed no sign of fear or awareness of the strange phenomenon, an unusual occurrence as dogs are intuitively psychic animals and often react defensively or fearfully in the presence of paranormal phenomena. Alison Smith's experience is much in the nature of a 'timeslip' haunting (see Chapter 6), where for a brief moment and through some unknown means, a living image of the past is momentarily superimposed over a present-day location. An actual instance of this taking place is included in a later part of this book. A place of human habitation and activity for nearly 1,000 years, perhaps it should be no surprise that some echo of this part of Stevenage's historic past somehow makes its presence felt again from time to time in the world of the living.

The pathway through the churchyard of St Nicholas' church, where Stevenage resident Alison Smith encountered a strange glowing vision of phantom people. (Paul Adams)

4

GHOSTS OF THE OLD TOWN

Henry Trigg and the Coffin in the Rafters

If you talk to anyone in Stevenage casually about the subject of ghosts and hauntings, invariably the name of Henry Trigg will come up at some point in the conversation. Trigg's macabre story has all the elements of a classic ghostly tale – grave-robbing, a mysterious will, a skeleton in an unburied coffin – and when this is combined with accounts of strange apparitions stirred into eerie life by renovations to ancient buildings it is no wonder that it has caught the imagination of several previous writers and researchers – Tony Broughall, Damien O'Dell, Ruth Stratton and Betty Puttick have all set down their own versions – and it remains the town's most well-known haunting.

Henry Trigg was a wealthy bachelor and successful local businessman and landowner from the first quarter of the eighteenth century. Middle Row, running north to south between Church Lane and the present-day Old Town High Street, was the site of Stevenage's first established centre of commerce with traders' shelters and permanent shops dating back to the 1200s. It was here that Trigg ran his butchers shop and grocery business and his standing within the community is evidenced by his other activities as warden of St Nicholas' church and general overseer of the parish. Henry also owned property and farmland including an orchard in the hamlets of Much Wymondley and Little Wymondley to the north of the town. Following his death in the autumn of 1724, Trigg, despite his not inconsiderable local achievements, would no doubt have sunk into obscurity had it not been for a specific clause in his now infamous will which was proved in the Archdeaconry of Huntingdon by his brother and executor, the Revd Thomas Trigg of Letchworth, on 15 October of the same year. Something of a local phenomenon, this document was still the cause of interest over a hundred years later when it was published complete under the title 'Eccentric Will' in *The Christian's Penny Magazine* of 21 February 1835. The cause of all the excitement was its opening paragraph with its novel and unconventional instructions as to the disposal of Trigg's mortal remains, here quoted in full:

I Henry Trigg of Stevenage, in the county of Hertford, being very infirm and weak in body, but of perfect sound mind and memory, praised be God for it, calling unto mind the mortality of my body, do now make and ordain this my last will and testament, in writing hereafter following; that is to say, principally I recommend my soul unto the merciful hands of Almighty God that first gave me it, assuredly believing and only expecting free pardon and forgiveness of all my sins, and eternal life in and through the only merits, death and passion of Jesus Christ my saviour; and as to my body, I commit it to the west end of my hovel, to be decently laid there, upon a floor erected by my executor, upon the purlins; upon the same purpose nothing doubting but at the general resurrection I shall receive the same again by the mighty power of God; and as for and concerning such worldly substance as it hath pleased God to bless me with this life, I do devise and dispose of the same in manner and form following.

Thomas Trigg, the principal beneficiary of his brother's will, had little choice but to follow Henry's instructions to the letter – failure to comply meant forfeiting his inheritance in favour of his younger brother George, who likewise would be passed over in favour of Henry Trigg's nephew William if he also felt disinclined to humour his uncle's bizarre request. Amid much local excitement, Trigg's body in its lead-lined coffin was lifted into the rafters of the barn behind his Middle Row shop, the eccentric grocer stipulating a minimum period of thirty years before any attempt was made to remove it. Shortly before his death, Trigg had been in negotiations with the parish authorities to rent the same barn for an annual sum of £1 10s for use as a public workhouse but his death before suitable renovations could be carried out meant that ultimately the deal was never completed.

According to tradition, Henry Trigg's fear of bodysnatching was at the root of his desire to establish a very public final resting place. An oft-quoted story describes how, returning home from a drinking session in the Black Swan tavern one dark night, Trigg and his two cronies were passing by a local churchyard when they came across a gang of grave robbers busily opening a recently filled-in grave. The sight of the Resurrectionists in action is said to have filled the old grocer with such horror that he made the decision then and there not to allow his own body to potentially suffer the same fate and came up with his decidedly unconventional burial plan. Interestingly, another Hertfordshire location with a ghost story and a rooftop 'coffin' is the manor house at Little Gaddesden near Berkhamsted. Here another churchwarden, William Jarman, is said to haunt the village pond where he committed suicide after allegedly being spurned by the daughter of Lord Bridgewater, but in this instance 'Jarman's Coffin' is actually a stone chimney feature rather than a real sepulchre and although the account of a haunting is well known, actual details of phenomena and its origins are difficult to pin down. As for Henry Trigg, his well-laid plan to beat the bodysnatchers was ultimately to prove a failure.

In 1774, fifty years after Henry Trigg's death, his former shop in Middle Row was converted into the Old Castle Inn and remained a hostelry until the early 1920s. On 10 July 1807, a disastrous fire broke out in a wheelwright's shop on the

Number 37 High Street, Stevenage Old Town – the former Old Castle Inn, for many years a branch of the NatWest bank. The famous coffin of Henry Trigg is in the roof of an outbuilding at the rear. (Paul Adams)

corner of Walkern Road which quickly spread to other buildings along the High Street. Trigg in his coffin avoided an unplanned cremation as the old barn was miraculously spared by the flames, but the Great Fire (one of several that took place during the early 1800s) destroyed many of the old timber shops and other structures, including hayricks and oasthouses. His remains had also narrowly escaped a conventional burial several years before when in 1769 a niece left 40s in her will for the coffin to be taken down and laid to rest in the normal way. Despite Henry's thirty-year proviso having by then expired, the continuing novelty of the body in the loft ensured that the request was never carried out.

Unfortunately for Henry Trigg, souvenir hunters were to succeed where the Resurrection men failed. When the original coffin, eroded by woodworm, was replaced with a new one in the early 1800s, the carpenter carried off a tooth and a lock of hair as a memento. In 1831, Mr Bellamy, the then landlord of the Old Castle, couldn't resist taking a peep inside and may have helped himself to a piece of Henry in the process. Bellamy claimed the body was intact and well preserved but by the time the East Herts Archaeological Society (founded in 1898) examined the coffin in the early 1900s they discovered that a third of the skeleton was missing. Further clandestine raids ensued causing further depletions, to the point that in order to cover their tracks and perpetuate the phenomenon of the rooftop relic, animal bones were substituted for the missing parts of the relic. In 1999, by which time Henry Trigg's former house, now listed as No.37 High Street, had become a branch of the NatWest bank, the old barn was repaired and the oak coffin with its lead cover was temporarily removed to an undertakers in Letchworth where restoration work was carried out. Whatever remains inside were finally laid to rest, 275 years after the original casket was hoisted into the rafters and this restored and now empty coffin continues to reside in its original location at the rear of the bank.

The famous coffin of Stevenage businessman and grocer Henry Trigg – his bones have long since vanished. (Paul Adams)

Not surprisingly, ghostly activity in and around this part of Stevenage Old Town has been put down to the unquiet spirit of the eccentric Henry Trigg. A common theme noted by ghost hunters and psychical researchers is the effect that building work and similar alterations can have on a particular building or location. An existing haunting may cease or become less active following structural alterations, or the opposite may happen and paranormal activity, including the sighting of apparitions and other phenomena such as poltergeist-like effects, may start up after a house, shop or other building is changed in some physical way.

In 1964, the Arrow Smith Engineering Works occupied premises adjacent to the old Trigg barn in Middle Row. In her book *Ghosts of Hertfordshire* (1994), the late Betty Puttick describes the experiences of Fred Usher, a builder employed to carry out renovation work in the Arrow Smith building. Fetching tools from a storeroom, Usher described seeing the apparition of a shabbily dressed man wearing old-fashioned gaiters who made no response to his enquiries and who seemed to drift away and disappear through a brick wall opposite. The wall into which the figure vanished was the party wall between the engineering works and Henry Trigg's barn with its eerily suspended coffin. Six years later, in May 1970, another apparition was seen, this time by builders converting the Old Castle Inn building into the current bank premises. Labourers on site reported a male figure dressed in a long striped apron that both appeared and disappeared in inexplicable circumstances. Another apparition, possibly the same one, was also seen on two occasions during the daytime in the

mid-1970s by employees of the Arrow Smith works. Today Henry Trigg's bones are long gone, but perhaps some intangible aspect of this extraordinary man can still be summoned back to the home he knew so well over three centuries ago.

Ghosts at the White Lion

Public houses and inns have been traditional meeting places providing shelter and company, as well as staging posts for travellers, for centuries, so it is no surprise that these buildings and their environs are some of the most commonly haunted buildings in the country. Ghosts appear in the oldest hostelries as well as in the newest. The Bingley Arms in the picturesque Yorkshire village of Bardsey is considered to be the oldest inn in England with a known history dating back to at least AD 953. Its ghosts include a phantom dog as well as the apparitions of a young woman and a Cavalier wearing a large-brimmed hat. In the mid-1990s, I met an architect involved in converting a former 1930s cinema in London into a new Wetherspoons pub, who told me that workmen on the site were refusing to go into one area of the building after one of the contractors claimed to have seen a headless figure in what had originally been the old projection room. Many of Hertfordshire's pubs have ghostly associations and here we will look at the haunted histories of a selection of Stevenage's hostelries.

A short walk from Middle Row and the eerie coffin of Henry Trigg is the White Lion public house, one of the Old Town's most notable historic buildings. Located on the corner of the High Street and Bell Lane, the current

The much-haunted White Lion pub, renamed The Mulberry Tree in 2015. Ghostly phenomena reported here include footsteps, swishing sounds and doors opening by themselves. (Paul Adams)

building dates from the eighteenth century but a coaching inn existed on the site before this time – an early landlord was William Welch who died in 1662 and who passed the business on to his daughter, Anne. The hostelry occupied an important position in the town, being adjacent to the regular cattle market, and was often frequented by butchers and drovers who plied their trade at the market sessions. At one time a large pond to the rear of the building was used to water the visiting beasts before they were moved on to be sold at auction.

By the middle of the 1700s, the White Lion comprised over 30 acres of land and boasted stabling for thirty horses. Most coaching inns of the period were built around a courtyard area accessed by a galleried gateway through which the coaches would pass to unload. Due to its age and the development of higher travelling coaches, the White Lion's gateway (in a part of the building which now no longer exists) was too low, with the result that passengers had to alight and depart from the roadway outside. This was a minor inconvenience and did not stop the inn from being one of the town's major staging posts and social centres. The gateway may have been in the section of the building which was destroyed in an outbreak of fire in 1804. The inn itself was fortunate to escape the ravages of the Great Fire of 1807, which – as has been mentioned – destroyed many buildings along the High Street and surrounding area.

Perhaps the White Lion's most dramatic association is with the fortunes of war, the Napoleonic Wars to be exact. Between 1796 and 1816 a purpose-built prisoner-of-war camp, the first of its kind in the world, was established by the Royal Navy Transport Board at Norman Cross near Peterborough in present-day Cambridgeshire, just over 40 miles due north of Stevenage, to hold captured French soldiers. Many of these Frenchmen found themselves marching through Stevenage where the White Lion was often used as an overnight staging post. The prisoners were held under heavy guard in the coaching inn's stables and outbuildings, and possibly in the tunnel (now blocked) which runs from the cellar of the pub under the road to the Cromwell Hotel at No.25 on the east side of the High Street. The present hotel dates from the middle of the eighteenth century but an earlier building on the site was once the home of John Thurloe (1616–1668), Secretary to the Council of State in Protectorate England and Spymaster to Oliver Cromwell.

Not surprisingly this connection with the times and emotions of the past has left more than just physical impressions on the fabric of the White Lion itself as much ghostly activity has been reported here (and continues to be experienced), making it one of the most continually haunted buildings, not only in the Old Town but in Stevenage as a whole. During their time at the pub, assistant managers Anya Ingarfill and Francesca Bartha have experienced a number of strange and unnerving happenings. Many times during the day and at night the sound of footsteps moving around the upper parts of the building where the staff accommodation is located have been heard by both women as well as other employees. Much of the phenomena reported from the White Lion is auditory in nature: scratching sounds, the sound of doors opening and closing in staff flats known to be empty at

the time, together with typical poltergeist-like banging and crashing noises. One particular sound heard on a number of occasions moving about was likened by Francesca to a rhythmic rustling or swishing noise, like the sleeves of a 'puffa jacket' rubbing against the material of the coat. On investigation the corridors and rooms were found to be empty. A lot of these happenings have been centred in one of the flats on the first floor over the bar area. On one occasion, as one of the bar staff was relaxing in the flat's living room, the room door opened by itself, stood open for several seconds and then quickly closed again. There were no accompanying sounds of movement as would be expected – the floorboards in this part of the building creak easily whenever someone walks about – and also, due to the marked slope of the floor and wall, it is impossible for the door into the room to swing open by itself: something would have had to physically push it open.

As well as the ghostly sounds, a partly enclosed beer garden area to the rear of the pub seems to be haunted on occasion by a glowing white shape that has

The White Lion pub – images taken from a CCTV video in the early hours of 18 July 2014 which seem to show a hazy white mass drifting amongst the chairs and tables. (Author's collection)

been seen several times as well as on one occasion being caught on a CCTV video camera. This remarkable incident took place on the night of 18 July 2014 during a lengthy thunderstorm which affected the region for several hours. Around 3.30 a.m., an external security camera recording black and white video footage picked up what appears to be a ball of glowing mist which 'materialises' amongst the tables and chairs left outside under a canopy and then drifts around for nearly twenty minutes before abruptly moving out of view and disappearing. I have examined several stills taken from the camera footage and one of these is reproduced on p.48. According to Anya and Francesca, a similar anomaly was seen in the same part of the premises two years previously. Like many reported paranormal photographs published on the Internet today, the White Lion 'ghost' may have a natural explanation, but it remains intriguing and there is no doubt that this old building has an undoubted psychic connection with the past. To much local consternation, the White Lion was renamed The Mulberry Tree by the Greene King brewery chain in early 2015.

The Royal Oak Hauntings

Pub managers Kai Gould and his brother Shayne are no strangers where encounters with the paranormal are concerned. During their time at The Station Hotel in Knebworth, both young men experienced strange and unusual happenings that left both convinced that they were sharing the living quarters of the hostelry with unseen presences. Much of the phenomena was in the nature of poltergeist-like activity: domestic appliances, including an electric kettle and a DVD player, would turn themselves on when neither of the Gould brothers were near them, while items were thrown about as though something was trying to attract attention. These included a toy teddy bear and a bunch of keys which were propelled from behind Kai as he sat alone in the living room of the flat and dropped on to the floor in front of him. On another occasion the shadowy figure of a male person was seen standing briefly at the end of a corridor. After leaving The Station Hotel, one would expect a new tenancy to be a welcome break from the mysterious world of the paranormal, but for Kai and Shayne the move to The Royal Oak in Walkern Road could well be described as jumping out of the proverbial frying pan into the paranormal fire …

Although a Victorian-era building now stands on the site, there has been a public house and inn here dating back to before the middle of the eighteenth century. The original Royal Oak was a timber building subsequently replaced which boasted a large paddock. According to historian Margaret Ashby, the Stevenage Vestry, an early incarnation of the Town Council, used the premises for official meetings during the period in the mid-1700s when the licensee was a local man named William Bennett. Where the origins of the haunting of The Royal Oak lie is unclear, particularly as the older pub building no longer exists. However, it seems possible that in some instances an actual location or the very ground itself is, for want of a better term, 'haunted' (and we will look at other examples and briefly at the issue of ley-lines in connection with psychic happenings in a later part of this book) with the result that whatever structure is erected on a particular spot will be affected in some way by psychical phenomena during the course of its lifetime.

From the outset The Royal Oak appeared to be alive with strange and at times unsettling activity. At first the phenomena was, as Kai Gould described to me, 'pretty intense', almost as though – having stored itself up over a period of time – it was allowed to release itself in the presence of suitably sensitive people. Shortly after moving into the pub, Kai was working decorating the kitchen when all the kitchen cupboards suddenly opened by themselves. Being alone at the time, the incident was understandably unnerving. Soon other members of staff began reporting unusual happenings. These included a cooking pan being thrown across the kitchen and mysterious

sounds and voices, with whispering noises and heavy breathing, as well as the sound of a little girl giggling to herself.

However, the haunting had made itself known to previous occupiers before the Gould brothers had moved in. In 2011, after closing time when the pub was locked, an assistant manager had two frightening personal experiences. Around one o'clock in the morning, while filling the fruit machines with change, she suddenly became aware of a presence standing next to her. Looking around it was clear that the bar area was completely empty, yet the feeling of an unseen person only a few inches away was practically overwhelming. The sensation lasted for several minutes before fading away. Soon after, again in the early hours of the morning, the same manager was standing in a corridor at the rear of the building when a door in front of her

The Royal Oak pub in Walkern Road, haunted by poltergeist-type phenomena and the apparition of a running man. (Paul Adams)

suddenly swung open by itself and she felt again an overwhelming sensation as if an invisible person had rushed past her in the darkness. Now terrified, her scream of alarm summoned other staff members sleeping in the flat upstairs but on investigation it was clear that all the external doors were locked and closed and there was simply no way that anyone could have got into that part of the building. It is possible that this running presence, which has been encountered on more than one occasion, is also a manifestation of a black male figure which has been seen several times walking around in the public bar areas.

According to Kai Gould, two people have died suddenly in the bar area in the past, a middle-aged man who collapsed and died in the 1960s, and another customer who again died apparently from a heart attack twenty years earlier. During a visit by a local medium some years before, it was alleged that a man had committed suicide in the hayloft of the original barn to the rear of the pub. Perhaps they are the presences, both seen and unseen, who make themselves known at The Royal Oak from time to time.

Footsteps at the Red Lion

The sound of disembodied footsteps is one of the most commonly reported instances of paranormal phenomena on record. There are numerous accounts in the literature of psychical research describing hauntings involving footfalls, footsteps and similar noises. Sometimes they are associated with other types of phenomena, such as the movement of objects and the appearance of apparitions, or in many cases the sound of an unseen person moving around is the only ghostly manifestation to be experienced. The duration of the phenomena can also vary from haunting to haunting, being either a regular occurrence that can stretch out over several months or even years, or alternatively a sudden and unexpected burst of activity that occurs once or twice and is never experienced again. An example of the former is the famous haunting of Borley Rectory where footsteps were heard inside the building by several of the incumbents over several decades as well as the year-long tenancy investigation by ghost hunter Harry Price in 1937 and 1938 (see my *The Borley Rectory Companion* (2009), pp.247–253); while a sudden and unexpected incident of ghostly footsteps (in this case the sound of hobnail boots walking across floorboards) was described to me by horror writer Guy N. Smith who experienced the unnerving incident (which occurred on one occasion only, like some sudden outburst of psychic energy) while working alone in his former flat in Lichfield.

Ghostly footsteps form the principal phenomena associated with the Red Lion, another of the Old Town's former coaching inns located on the west side of the High Street close to the junction with Drapers Way. An impressive building which retains its galleried courtyard entrance, the building dates from the seventeenth century and like many old buildings was refaced with brickwork in Victorian times, giving it an appearance which belies its real age. At one point the Red Lion was one of several hostelries in the area owned by John Pryor, a successful brewer and entrepreneur from nearby Baldock who bought the building in 1821.

Many of the bar staff have experienced the sound of people moving around inside the pub, both upstairs in the living areas as well in the ground-floor bar. The sound of footsteps are also accompanied at times by the sound of doors opening and closing although on investigation nothing is found to have been moved or put out of place. According to the staff I spoke to during a visit to the Red Lion in the summer of 2014, the footsteps are heard on a regular basis, normally every two weeks or so, as if some kind of psychic energy is able to build up and then release itself. A former manager named Mandy had an unnerving encounter while alone in the rear customer area one day. Standing by the bar she heard the unmistakable sound of heavy footsteps coming towards her across the room from the direction of the toilets at the rear of the building. The footfalls, which were slow and deliberate, seemed to reach the middle of the room and suddenly stop. Nothing was visible at all during the experience. Perhaps the unseen visitor was the unquiet spirit of the ubiquitous John Pryor who regularly returns to this ancient building, unwilling to relinquish a hold on part of his extensive empire of inns and brewery houses?

The Red Lion pub in the Old Town High Street, where phantom footsteps have been heard. (Paul Adams)

The Roebuck Highwayman

The famous highwayman Dick Turpin, hanged in York at the age of 33 for horse theft on 7 April 1739, has become one of England's most romantic and legendary figures. He has also become a much-travelled ghost as there are a number of buildings and locations around the country where his unquiet spirit is said to return from time to time. Perhaps the most bizarre location for a haunting by Turpin is the main terminal at Heathrow Airport where a figure wearing a tricorn hat and long horse coat has allegedly been encountered. Turpin is also said to haunt the Old Manor in Bracknell High Street in Berkshire, where a portion of the building was once known as 'Dick Turpin's Cottage', as well as Epping Forest in Essex and Woughton on the Green in Buckinghamshire where a dark figure mounted on a horse is thought to be none other than the daring – and in reality brutal – brigand. In 1947, a Mr Key living in a house known as 'Woodfield' in Weathercock Lane in Aspley Guise, Bedfordshire, applied to Luton Borough Council for a reduction in his rates (Council Tax in modern parlance) due to the fact that the value of his house was being reduced due to the local belief that it was haunted by Dick Turpin's ghost. A spectral figure, thought to be that of Turpin himself, had apparently been seen dismounting from an equally ghostly horse and entering the garden at a place no longer used as an entrance. Despite being investigated by members of the Society for Psychical Research, the claim and a subsequent appeal were dismissed by the Bedfordshire Quarter Sessions Appeals Committee.

The historic Roebuck Inn, said to have been visited by highwayman Dick Turpin. (Paul Adams)

The historic Roebuck Inn, now used as both a traditional public house and a hotel, is also – according to local legend – a place where Dick Turpin is said to have visited at some point in his lifetime. This attractive building dates from the fifteenth century with later sixteenth and seventeenth-century additions, so ancient even by the time the real Dick Turpin was making a name for himself across the country. Whether Turpin actually stayed here is now impossible to ascertain, as is whether he is the unseen presence felt and sometimes heard on the staircase leading up from the ground-floor bar area. I have spoken with guests who claimed to have heard footsteps on the stairs but perhaps understandably, members of staff were unwilling to discuss the haunting with me during a visit in 2014. Some establishments consider ghosts are good for business and others do not.

A Friendly Phantom

Not all of Stevenage's pub ghosts are sinister shades or violent poltergeist-like entities. A final hostelry haunting involving a gentle and somewhat friendlier ghost is that associated with The Marquis of Lorne, a former brick-fronted cottage and brew-house that in the late 1700s was owned by a publican named Joseph Emery. During the interwar years, The Marquis of Lorne was a popular restaurant that catered for visiting cyclists on day-trips from London. Amy, one of the bar staff at the pub today, described to me what appears to be a gentle ghost who moves items around behind the bar and in the kitchen areas. There appears to be nothing unpleasant or frightening about this particular haunting and staff have accepted it as part of the overall charm of the building itself. During a clairvoyant evening some years ago it was

The Roebuck Inn – the staircase where an invisible presence has been felt. (Paul Adams)

A friendly ghost and the sound of a skipping child have been heard by staff at The Marquis of Lorne pub in the Old Town High Street. (Paul Adams)

suggested that the upper floor of the building was haunted by the ghost of a young man who may also be the same spirit who makes his presence known downstairs from time to time. Staff have also heard the sound of light running footsteps, like a small skipping child, on occasions in the upper part of the building.

Tale of the Brown Man

We have already encountered the ghostly history of the White Lion, one of Old Stevenage's most notable coaching inns. During the heyday of long-distance horse-drawn travel, another hostelry of similar importance was The Swan, located at the extreme northern periphery of the High Street. One of The Swan's most notable visitors was the famous diarist Samuel Pepys (1633–1703), who stayed here on more than one occasion and enjoyed a game of bowls with his travelling companions on the green that at one time stood opposite the inn. Pepys knew the town well as at one time his father, John Pepys, owned a house here. The Swan is known to have had an underground passage connected to one of its buildings, which has given rise to the legend that at one time it was used as a hideout by Dick Turpin. This passageway, which survived into the twentieth century, appears to have been blocked up in the 1940s.

The Grange, formerly The Swan Inn, where the apparition of a man in brown has been seen. (Paul Adams)

As an inn, The Swan itself was still trading in the mid-nineteenth century, but in 1847 it was put up for sale and was subsequently bought by the Revd John Osborne Seager, a local philanthropist, who renamed it The Grange and set about converting the buildings into a preparatory school. Seager served as headmaster until 1883 when he was succeeded by his son, another cleric, the Revd John Lingen Seager. During the First World War, The Grange was used by a local war works department to make field bandages and dressings, while in the Second World War it operated as a school for evacuees under the control of Hertfordshire County Council. The post-war years saw The Grange being put to a variety of uses, including the town Registry Office, a children's home, as well as council offices. Today the entire building has been converted into residential apartments. Much of the building that can be seen today dates from the 1700s, although an interesting feature often overlooked is the front portico where columns originally formed a gallery at the west end of St Nicholas' church which were subsequently taken down in the nineteenth century.

With such an involved history, The Grange deserves more of a haunted history than it currently enjoys. There are two ghosts associated with the building, a whispering woman who haunts the site of one of the old staircases, and the figure of a man dressed in a brown tunic, said to be a former stableman from the coaching days of The Swan Inn. This particular phantom is said to have been seen by a caretaker in broad daylight in the mid-1960s during the time that the building was being used as the Briar Patch Children's Home. When approached the figure simply vanished but had previously appeared solid and lifelike. Perhaps the many alterations and changes that have taken place on the site down through the years have, as can be the case with haunted buildings, changed the psychic fabric to such an extent that now whatever phenomena once occurred here has finally run its course. Whether new ghosts will walk The Grange in future years remains to be seen.

5

THE STEVENAGE POLTERGEIST

Some Classic Poltergeist Hauntings

Fear of the unknown makes the subject of ghosts and haunting a taboo one for many people, but perhaps the most frightening of all supernatural phenomena, even for ghost hunters and believers in the paranormal, is that associated with the poltergeist. Poltergeist is a German word variously translated as 'noise spirit', 'noisy ghost' or 'knocking ghost'. Characterised by the often violent movement and destruction of objects, poltergeist activity has been recorded over the course of several hundred years and, unlike traditional haunting which are essentially restricted to a particular location or environment – most often a haunted house or building – poltergeists are person-focused haunting which take place around and in the presence of a particular family member (described as the 'nexus' of the haunting), most often an adolescent youth or teenager. One of the earliest cases to display poltergeist-type phenomena occurred in Ravenna, Italy, in AD 530. The first British case of which a detailed account survives took place in North Aston in Oxfordshire in 1591 when, according to reports, stones were thrown around and seen to fall from the ceiling of a farmhouse belonging to a Mr George Lee and his family.

In recent times there have been several high-profile poltergeist cases, both in this country and abroad, which have created newspaper headlines and controversy in equal measure. In 1967, German parapsychologist Hans Bender (1907–1991) investigated the Rosenheim Poltergeist of Southern Bavaria. In the ordinary working office of a practicing solicitor named Sigmund Adam, bizarre and seemingly inexplicable happenings, including the swinging of corridor light fittings, telephones ringing by themselves together with multiple calls being placed to the automated speaking clock (sometimes as many as four in one minute, a physical impossibility using the office handsets of the time) took place in the presence of Herr Adam's 19-year-old secretary, Annemarie Schaberl. Fräulein Schaberl, an unhappy woman who disliked her job, eventually left the practice, bringing the Rosenheim Poltergeist case to an end.

During the summer of 1979, a lawnmower repair workshop in Cardiff became the playground of 'Pete the Poltergeist', a lively ghost who, as well as throwing numerous stones, made objects appear in people's pockets and caused tools to materialise in mid-air and fall to the floor. The case was investigated by the late David Fontana, a highly respected member of the Society for Psychical Research (SPR) who became convinced that the phenomena was genuine. One witness claimed to have encountered 'Pete' himself, the apparition of a small boy who he claimed he saw sitting on a beam high up in the workshop roof. However, probably the most famous and controversial modern poltergeist case of the past forty years, and one which continues to arouse interest today, took place in a small council house in the north London suburb of Enfield in the late 1970s. For a period of over a year, beginning in the late August of 1977, the Hodgson family – Mrs Peggy Hodgson together with her four children, 13-year-old Rose, 10-year-old Peter, Janet aged 11 and her 7-year-old brother, Jimmy – were subjected to a wild and frightening assault which turned the house in Green Street into a paranormal bedlam: objects flew through the air, doors slammed by themselves and the children were pulled out of their beds and 'levitated', as if by unseen hands. The Enfield Poltergeist made front-page headlines in the *Daily Mirror* newspaper and a subsequent book on the case by one of its lead investigators, Guy Lyon Playfair, became a bestseller, eventually running to several editions. The disturbances finally died down in October 1978 with a final brief resurgence of a very mild

Destruction of physical objects experienced during a poltergeist outbreak, in this instance the Runcorn Poltergeist in the early 1950s. (Peter Underwood Collection/Paul Adams)

DAILY Mirror

BRITAIN'S BIGGEST DAILY SALE   7p   Saturday, September 10, 1977

The house of strange happenings

By GEORGE FALLOWS and DOUGLAS BENCE

A FAMILY is living in fear of strange goings-on that are driving them from their home.

For two weeks, they have been terrorised by objects inexplicably shooting through the air, or furniture moving for no apparent reason.

Two clergymen have blessed the house, but the happenings have only increased. Police are baffled by the phenomena, and one policewoman is too scared to return to the house.

For four days, Mirror reporters George Fallows and Douglas Bence and photographers David Thorpe and Graham Morris joined a psychic expert in keeping watch.

They have witnessed events they cannot explain.

In the last eight days, a saucer has jumped across the kitchen, furniture has moved and marbles and toy building bricks have shot through the air in the 60-year-old house at Enfield, Middlesex.

Knocks

One brick hit Morris on the head.

Children's story books in a bedroom were seen to fly through the air by friends of the family.

Police heard knockings which they could not explain, and a policewoman saw a chair move on its own.

Fallows says: "Having kept observation at the house for four successive nights I believe abnormal happenings are occurring.

"I have seen nothing unusual, but I have heard knocks, and I've been present when strange occurrences have been witnessed by others in a back bedroom."

Photographer Morris

Terror for family in spook riddle

says: "I was sent to what I was told was a haunted house.

"When I went into the living room I saw toy bricks flying through the air. One of them hit me on the head.

"Nobody seemed to be throwing them. They were coming at the speed of bullets.

"I saw at least three and attempted to photograph them—but they were too fast for me."

Hit

Reporter Bence says: "I saw a yellow brick hit the wall where I lost it in the flash from Morris's camera.

"I did not see the brick that hit him on the head and missed a third that others saw."

In an effort to unravel the mystery, the Daily Mirror called in Mr. Maurice Grosse, a member of the Society for Psychical Research, one of the most reput-

able organisations in the field.

Mr. Grosse said: "I believe that genuine poltergeist-type phenomena is occurring, but it does not mean it is a haunted house.

"This type of manifestation is attached to people, not places."

Shortly after Mr. Grosse began to investigate, a ten-year-old son of the family returned to residential school and the strange happenings ceased.

For 48 hours nothing unusual took place, then on Wednesday night a ten-year-old girl reported that a marble had "flown through the air" in her bedroom.

Bump

Mr. Grosse and Fallows returned to the house.

They were joined by Bence and Thorpe.

In the early hours of Thursday, they heard a bump and found a book, which had been on the mantelpiece in the girl's bedroom, was on the floor. They replaced it.

A few minutes later, they heard another

'I saw toy bricks go shooting across a room'

Continued on Page Two ◇

Ho Sh so By squ

THE rebel so Shore was fo hours after a

And last nigh 21-year-old Pier where she lives.

The girl, Jayne just two months

SQUATTER: Jayn her derelict h

Typical popular press coverage of a poltergeist haunting, in this instance the famous Enfield Poltergeist from 1977. (UKPressOnline)

nature lasting only a few days ending in April the following year. Interest in the case remains high, with a high-profile television adaptation of *The Enfield Haunting* starring Timothy Spall appearing in May 2015.

Poltergeists are one area of the paranormal that continue to divide researchers as to their nature and causes. For many years it was thought that the physical phenomena associated with poltergeist cases was due to some form of externalisation of telekinetic (i.e. mind over matter) energy created by the often young and adolescent subjects around which the hauntings are centred. This still remains true for some investigators. However, some researchers and commentators, such as Guy Playfair and the late Colin Wilson, have come to the conclusion that rather than being random and uncontrolled outbursts, the 'energy' involved is actually being manipulated by distinct individual personalities (discarnate 'spirits' or 'entities' for want of better words) which are able to spontaneously latch on to and feed off of the forces involved.

Bedlam in Byron Close

In May 2012 a curious thirty-minute video film was posted on the popular media-sharing website YouTube by South London-based filmmaker, Richard Corbelli. Titled *The Stevenage Poltergeist*, it documented over a period of three days from 15–17 February 2010 the investigation and 'clearing' or banishment of a destructive poltergeist haunting that had apparently been taking place in an ordinary 1970s-built semi-detached house in the Chells

district of Stevenage. The homeowners, a retired couple named Allen and Ivy, had seemingly experienced months of violent and destructive phenomena including broken windows and smashed ornaments and furniture; water had poured in torrents from the loft, the house was regularly filled with an inexplicable and unpleasant atmosphere, light fittings were pulled from the walls and ceilings, and an ordinary sofa was said to have moved by itself and been seen floating several inches off of the floor. At the centre of the disturbances was their 15-year-old grandson Jason who had been forced to leave his mother Debbie's house nearby after similar activity had resulted in the local authority giving the family an ultimatum that either the destruction being caused to the property ceased or they would be thrown out of the house.

According to Jason himself, interviewed on camera by Corbelli during the course of his stay at Byron Close, the phenomena had begun with the novel and mysterious disappearance of food from his dinner plate during the course of family meals. Soon food was being propelled and thrown around the room (with Jason's mother Debbie a popular target) by apparently unseen hands, marking the beginning of numerous and increasingly destructive happenings that continued with no sign of abating for over a year. With his mother (a single parent) remaining in her own home, Jason had moved in with his grandparents, Allen and Ivy, who themselves had lived in Byron Close for twenty-six years, but it wasn't long before similar poltergeist-like activity began transforming their ordinary suburban dwelling into a paranormal war zone. Allen had run his own business for several years while Ivy worked part-time as an operator in a police control room. Soon household items and pieces of furniture, including coffee tables, lamps, ornaments, jewellery and computer parts, began to be hurled around to the point that, to prevent further damage, many items were removed from the house and stored in a large summer house at the bottom of the garden for safekeeping.

Call in the Ghostbusters

With the seemingly inexplicable happenings showing no sign of abating, the events at Byron Close eventually came to the attention of Mia Dolan, an author and experienced psychic medium who had recently achieved a level of success as a regular contributor to the *Haunted Homes* television series. Together with paranormal investigators Mark Webb and Andy Matthews, and sceptical researcher Chris French, Professor of Psychology at Goldsmiths, University of London, Mia had been filmed visiting allegedly haunted houses and buildings around the country in an attempt to both capture evidence of psychic phenomena as well as bringing frightening and unpleasant incidents affecting the occupiers to a close. The programme lasted two series and has subsequently been released on DVD. At Stevenage and accompanied by several members of Manchester Paranormal, an investigative group, together with Mia's partner Craig, an electronics and surveillance specialist, Mia visited the house on several occasions, her final visit involving an elaborate ritual which she claimed would drive the haunting element from the house, much of which forms the basis for Richard Corbelli's video film.

Byron Close, scene of the extraordinary case of the Stevenage Poltergeist. (Paul Adams)

While researching this particular case I was immensely fortunate to get in touch not only with Richard Corbelli, whose film footage forms an essential part of the documentation, but also with Chris Body, a paranormal researcher who spent two full days and an afternoon with the family and was able to personally experience what he later described to me as being some of the most extraordinary incidents he, together with the members of Manchester Paranormal, have ever encountered. Like a number of people whose experiences with the paranormal are included in the present book, Chris has been aware of paranormal influences from a young age, while a decision in later life to contact a medium in the hope of trying to find some explanation for his experiences ultimately brought him in touch with Mia Dolan. When Mia requested that he assist her and the members of Manchester Paranormal – brothers Peter, Darren and David Sarsfield, plus Ian Landrigan and freelance cameraman, Lloyd Pennington – at a 'house sit' at an investigation 30 miles north of London, Chris had no idea that this would bring him into direct contact with the case of the Stevenage Poltergeist.

On 10 February 2015, I held an hour-long interview with Chris on the telephone and heard first-hand his own personal account of his extraordinary visit to Byron Close. Striking physical phenomena took place at the very outset. As soon as the car pulled up in the street outside the house, a stone suddenly bowled across the road, seemingly from out of nowhere, and landed with astonishing accuracy on the side of Chris' shoe. Stone throwing is a remarkably consistent phenomenon reported in numerous poltergeist hauntings across the world as well as down through the years from the first accounts for which records exist. The unexpected incident was an indicator of much of what was to take place at Byron Close during the next few days.

Inside the house, Chris was able to see the results of months of what appeared to be relentless and brutal psychical activity. Many of the rooms were semi-bare with dents and holes in the walls. Despite it being a hot summer day, all the curtains were pulled and the windows closed. The family members – Jason, Allen and Ivy – were sleeping on the floor in what appeared to be very basic and frugal circumstances, apparently having been thrown out of bed on a number of occasions. Mia Dolan, who was working with the family to bring the alarming events to a close, was already at the property, as was young Jason who Chris described to me as, despite the wanton destruction and suspension of normality, particularly enjoying the level of attention that the poltergeist haunting brought to him. There were no electrical appliances apart from a kettle; all items that were light enough to be thrown about had been moved to the shed at the bottom of the garden with only heavy pieces of furniture remaining. Everyone drank from plastic cups and once the kettle had boiled for tea, Ivy habitually threw away the remaining hot water in case the poltergeist decided to throw it at one or more of the visitors. Similarly, all plates and cutlery were cardboard and plastic and both grandparents, who were heavy smokers, used light tinfoil ashtrays.

Days and Nights in a Haunted House

During his time at Byron Close, Chris Body soon discovered that the daylight hours were the time when the most spectacular phenomena would take place. Little or no activity was reported during the night-time, although on a number of occasions Chris found scratch marks on his back and arms upon waking, which he could not account for. Not long after arriving, Chris spent some time sitting in the conservatory at the back of the house. After around ten to fifteen minutes, a stone struck the window directly behind his head, showering glass on to the floor. As far as he could tell, everyone had been inside the house at the time and it would have been impossible for anyone outside to have thrown a stone so that it could hit the window pane at such an angle.

Later the same afternoon, Chris, together with Jason and two other members of the Manchester group, went out to the local fish and chip shop which was around a ten minute walk from the house. As the group walked along the street, stones seemed to fall out of the sky and strike the ground with such force that they ricocheted off the pavement, hitting the sides of several parked cars. Although Jason would seem to be the obvious culprit, Chris Body was and remains convinced that the young lad did not cheat and that the stones appeared as if from nowhere, as if the poltergeist had somehow saved them up and was now releasing them at random. Jason was in clear view all the time and the two researchers from Manchester had purposely arranged to walk on either side with Chris at the rear.

Following a quiet night, similar inexplicable activity took place at intervals throughout the next day. At one point Ian Landigan complained of being forcibly pulled off the sofa by his ankle on to the living room floor; taps were found running and on several occasions a weird Arabic-style writing was found scrawled on sections of wall known to have been previously untouched. During this time the researchers, together with Chris, had purposely been keeping Jason as well as his grandparents under observation. All were convinced that none of the family present could have been responsible for the 'phenomena'.

Later the same day a particularly striking incident took place. As part of their investigation, the Manchester group had placed a number of 'trigger objects' around the house with the express intention of stimulating the poltergeist to move or disturb them in some way. A number of these objects were small plastic ducks which could be easily seen. During a break in the vigil, several members of the group together with Jason went out to a nearby kebab shop. After being served with food, Chris opened one of the polystyrene burger boxes and was stunned to find one of the small plastic duck toys nestling amongst the chips. Could Jason have slipped the item in without being seen? All members present were convinced that, like the stones falling from the sky the previous day, Jason had been under observation the whole time and that to have faked the effect would have been impossible.

The second and final day at Byron Close was marked with several further incidents of stone throwing. When examined, the stones were found to be cobbles which appeared to have been pulled out of the edge of the driveway at the front of the house. At one point, as Lloyd Pennington was bringing several pieces of equipment in from the team's van which was parked on the driveway, a cobblestone suddenly flew past Chris Body's head and struck the side of the van with considerable force. Only the two men were present at the time – the stone appeared to have again been propelled from out of nowhere.

Driving Out the Darkness

Following a break of several weeks, the Manchester Paranormal team together with Mia Dolan returned to Byron Close with the object of finally bringing the disturbances to an end. This part of the investigation forms the subject of Richard Corbelli's YouTube film and readers are invited to find and watch this and see what they make of the case for themselves. During the intervening period the disturbances had died down somewhat and it appears that the most violent and dramatic stages of the haunting had in fact passed. However, odd things still continued to take place in and around the house. At one point a loud clattering sound was heard coming from the conservatory roof when all members of the team and the family were inside. This proved to be a pot Buddha ornament which had struck the roof and ended up lying in the garden. On another occasion a cigarette lighter was seen to be thrown from one side of a bedroom to the other.

While at the house, Mia carried out what could be described as a 'clearing' ritual involving a large circle marked out with sage, rock salt and holy water on the hallway floor with the intention of forcing whatever malign forces were active inside to leave. A similar ritual was also undertaken in Jason's mother's house. After this the atmosphere inside the house was noticeably different and apart from a few small incidents which took place on a follow-up visit two months later, the haunting at the time of writing (February 2015) appears to have come to an end.

Can we explain these bizarre and at times distressing and frightening events? For those not personally involved it is easy to dismiss such happenings in various ways – hysteria, fraud, frightened fancy and the will to believe. Those involved in investigating the case of the Stevenage Poltergeist came away from it convinced as to the reality of paranormal forces and their ability to manifest in the material world. Chris Body is convinced that what he and his friends encountered during their time at Byron Close was some form of 'entity' or discarnate personality that for a time was able to act through Jason himself. This brief chapter is the first to be written about this remarkable case and it is to be hoped that a more detailed account will appear from those involved sometime in the future as it deserves to be preserved for posterity. Out of respect for the family involved I have not included any photographs as illustrations – those wishing to find out more can check out Richard Corbelli's 'The Stevenage Poltergeist' online.

6

NEW TOWN HAUNTINGS AND OTHER STRANGE STORIES

A Child in the Night

Hauntings that involve children or the appearance of child ghosts can be both poignant and unsettling, particularly if the impression is of lost or wandering spirits and apparitions. There are a number of locations and buildings around the country said to be haunted by children or child-like phantoms. In 2014, there were several reported sightings of the so-called 'black-eyed' child ghosts in the vicinity of lonely Cannock Chase in Staffordshire, scene of a series of notorious child murders in the mid-1960s. The figure of a bare-footed girl in a white party dress was seen by two witnesses in Drury Lane, Houghton Regis, in the early 1970s, while the Old Coach House at Hatfield in Hertfordshire is haunted by the figure of an unknown girl who has been seen playing happily in one of the rooms – often mistaken for a real child, when approached the girl simply vanishes. At Bramber Castle in West Sussex, two wretched children,

emaciated and dressed in rags, have been glimpsed from time to time, often at Christmas time, amongst the castle ruins. They are thought to be the sons of William de Braose who, along with William's wife, were starved to death in Windsor Castle by King John in the early thirteenth century. At the Tower of London, the White Tower is said to be haunted by two small fleeting figures that appear hand-in-hand dressed in white nightgowns. Around 1483, the young Edward V together with Richard, Duke of York, disappeared in mysterious circumstances, believed murdered. The fates of the so-called 'Princes in the Tower' has never been solved, but these occasionally sighted apparitions may well be a psychic echo of a cruel and violent past.

Not all child ghosts, however, haunt stately homes and crumbling castles, as the following modern accounts clearly demonstrate. Valley Way, separated from Monks Wood and Whormeley Wood by a large playing field, runs north–south between the Six Hills Way and the A602 dual-carriageway on the south-east side of Stevenage. It was here that three members of the Harrison family had an unsettling experience in their own home around 2010. One Saturday night, Jackie Harrison's 14-year-old daughter, together with a school friend staying in the house for a sleepover, were disturbed in the early hours of the morning by what appeared to be the voice of a crying child. Both girls woke at exactly 3.00 a.m. and heard the sound of a young girl sobbing and crying out the words, 'Daddy, help me. Please help me ...' The voice appeared to be coming from behind a wooden fence at the bottom of the garden which backed on to the open field bordering Monks Wood, but was so distinct that it could be heard clearly inside the bedroom. Understandably scared, the two girls woke Jackie but by the time she went into her daughter's bedroom the crying voice had stopped. Dismissing it either as a dream or a prank, Jackie Harrison ignored the girls' protests and went back to bed.

The following Saturday the Harrisons' daughter was away from home on another sleepover. Perhaps not surprisingly given the recent strange events – and unconvinced by Jackie's explanations – the daughter's friend had vowed not to stay over at Valley Way again. That evening, following an argument with her husband, Jackie Harrison chose to sleep by herself in her daughter's bedroom. Restless and unable to sleep, she lay awake for some time until she suddenly became aware of sobbing that appeared to be coming from somewhere outside the house. Like her daughter and her friend the previous weekend, she could hear a young child that she described to the present writer as seeming to belong to a girl aged around 10 years. The child was crying pitifully

and repeating over and over again, 'Daddy, help me. Please help me ...' Frightened, Jackie got up and looked out through the window but the garden and the field beyond was in darkness. The time on the bedroom clock showed exactly 3.00 a.m. Eventually the sounds gradually faded away but strangely had been clear enough to be heard along the upstairs landing and in her own bedroom where her husband lay asleep. She estimated that the whole episode had lasted around five minutes.

Convinced that the sounds were not due to people in the house next door (the property is an end of terrace house) or someone in the field opposite, Jackie Harrison decided the following Saturday to set her alarm for ten minutes before three in order to try and hear the mysterious voice again. However, despite waking at the appointed time the eerie voice did not manifest and none of the Harrison family have heard the crying child again. To date there have been no further paranormal incidents connected with the household. It seems that this was a curious random incident as some accounts of ghostly activity prove to be. Who the child was, why she was seemingly lost or distressed, and how her sad and unhappy voice came to be heard by complete strangers on two specific occasions over the course of a week remains, like many of the cases in this book, a strange enigma.

A Haunted Cottage

A less distressing account of a child haunting is connected with Dane Cottage, a Victorian-era house located a short distance away from Valley Way in London Road directly opposite the Royal Mail Delivery Office. A former owner discussed her experiences with me, which included the appearance of a little girl who was often seen several times sitting at the top of the stairs. With her old-fashioned pinafore dress and hairstyle her appearance was likened to the illustrations which at one time were used to advertise Pear's Soap in the 1930s. At Dane Cottage the haunting was a light-hearted one as if the ghostly child was intent on having fun at the owner's expense and there was no trace of the sadness often associated with hauntings of this nature. Small household items and ornaments were often found moved out of position or transported into different rooms and there is a possibility that the phenomena may have involved a second child ghost, that of a small boy. As well as the appearance of an apparition, the family also experienced unusual sounds likened to the moving of furniture which were heard coming from upstairs rooms known to be unoccupied at the time, while a paper-shredding machine would often turn on and off by itself.

Like a Living Person

The following two accounts of ghostly activity, despite taking place in modern buildings, occurred in reasonably close proximity to St Nicholas' church and the old centre of Stevenage that we have already encountered earlier in this book. The first took place in 1972 in a house in Canterbury Way which forms the centre of a large New Town development known aptly as the St Nicholas Estate. Margaret Lonsdale moved to Stevenage from Chester le Street, Co. Durham, as an 18 year old in 1968. In 1973 she married Mick Hughes, who himself had

also arrived in the town with his father from Twickenham in West London in 1966 aged 16. The couple have been together ever since and both have experienced a number of interesting and at times unsettling encounters with the paranormal during that time, some of which they have allowed me to publish in this book for the first time.

Bob Dines was a local man who lived in a house in Canterbury Way. Unbeknown to Margaret Hughes at the time, Dines' children had seen the ghostly figure of a woman appear in their room at night standing looking down at them as they lay in their beds. Visiting the family one day, Margaret remembers sitting alone in the ground-floor living room while Bob and his children were all in the kitchen adjacent. At one point the room door opened and Margaret looked up to see a woman standing in the doorway looking intently at her. She was dressed in clothes that matched the fashion of the period – the early 1970s – and had dark-coloured hair. The figure was so real and lifelike that at that moment she was convinced that it was a real person. Strangely, the visitor remained completely silent, continued to stare at her for a short time and then suddenly was no longer there.

Disturbed by the incident, Margaret soon established that there was no one matching that description either living in the house or due to visit that day. In fact, it would have been impossible for a person to step into the room the way the woman had as she would have had to pass through the kitchen where Bob Dines and his family were standing. The identity of the woman and what she wanted that day have never been solved. Over the years since that time, Margaret has had a number of similar experiences of seeing apparitions and ghostly figures, which seems to suggest a close affinity with the world of the unseen. While on holiday several years later at the Beach Station Caravan Park in Felixstowe, Margaret saw on more than one occasion the figure of a woman with blond hair 'like Lady Diana' who appeared sitting in one of the window seats. On each occasion when she tried to draw her husband's attention to the figure it quickly vanished.

Like the woman who opened the door in Canterbury Way, the caravan lady was also solid and realistic. Other ghosts that Margaret Hughes has seen have not been so distinct. On another occasion, while in a hotel in the North of England, Margaret recalls waking in the night to see the figure of a woman wearing decidedly old-fashioned clothes looking down intently at her sleeping husband from the bedside. The apparition was very much transparent in appearance but what struck Margaret the most was the absolute look of joy on the lady's face, as though she was delighted to have been able to come into contact with someone from the world of the living again. As Margaret watched, the woman suddenly seemed to 'burst like a bubble' and was gone. Are these apparitions the actual spirits of the dead who live on in a parallel realm which is at the same time both inconceivably remote yet seemingly lies just within the reach of those with the psychic gift (like Margaret Hughes) to obtain glimpses through the veil? If so then it seems that, like moths clustering around a light or flame, these ghosts are instantly attracted when in the presence of someone endowed with the ability to acknowledge their presence.

A typical recreation of a haunting apparition. In reality many phantom figures appear like solid living people such as the woman seen by Margaret Hughes in Canterbury Way. (Author's collection)

Shadows From the Past

The 1881 Ordnance Survey map of the area around St Nicholas gives an idea of the rural tranquillity that once existed here and which is difficult to imagine was at one time a part of real life. The same is true for any area of the country which has out of necessity become part of modern urban development. The line of the present-day Weston Road can be made out as it heads north to the now obliterated hamlet of Rook's Nest (home at one time to novelist E.M. Forster) although the large chalk pit at its southerly end is now part of new houses in St Albans Drive. The entire St Nicholas estate was built on open farmland, including the numerous tributaries of York Road which lie to the south of Canterbury Way where we have seen Margaret Hughes had her encounter

with a dramatic and lifelike apparition. Something of the past, an echo or some form of trace memory or vibration of former times, seems to linger on here as the testimony of Alison Smith (who was born in Stevenage in 1958 and who we have already met in connection with her experience in St Nicholas' churchyard) clearly shows.

Alison's experiences are at the same time unusual and distinctly disturbing. On numerous occasions over a period of several years, she and her family were disturbed by the appearance of vague shadowy shapes 'like pillars of smoke' which seemed to flit or drift across one particular corner of the ground-floor front room, as though a crowd of indistinct people were passing by. These impressions were accompanied at differing times by noises that were likened to the movement or sounds of animals moving past, as one

York Road in the St Nicholas area of Stevenage, where mysterious misty apparitions and the sounds of animals have been heard. (Paul Adams)

might expect a herd or flock would make if it were being herded by a drover in some far-off day. The noises, which Alison and her family found impossible to reproduce, were most often heard in one of the first-floor bedrooms.

What is of interest here is that both Alison's home and that of their next-door neighbour appeared to share the same haunting as the house on the other side of the party wall was also affected by a similar visual phenomenon. On occasion the downstairs rooms were suddenly filled with shapes or shadows that did not seem to belong to either the people living there or the room's contents. It is difficult not to feel that this curious haunting was in some way connected with the ancient days of Stevenage's past, possibly an echo of rural life that at one time took place in the open countryside that many centuries later would be changed drastically by the expansion of the New Town development. Alison Smith herself told me that she felt the house was located on the former course of an old trackway, possibly a drovers' road, along which people and beasts passed on a regular basis in days gone by. It would be interesting to know whether other houses in the same area were or are affected by similar phenomena.

A Curious Happening at Sishes Mansion

Towards the end of his life, the great English ghost-story writer Montague Rhodes (M.R.) James (1862–1936) was asked by a friend what his views were on the subject of hauntings and the supernatural. James was emphatic when he replied: 'Depend upon it. Some of these things are so, but we do not know the rules.' This concisely sums up what we know (or do not know) about the paranormal today. That people see ghosts or experience paranormal or psychical phenomena is clearly demonstrated by the wealth of evidence recorded over many years (centuries in fact) that is available to read, research and study. But the controlling factors – what actually make these experiences and phenomena occur – is still at present beyond our understanding. Some hauntings can last for years; others flare up and can last a few weeks or even days and then disappear never to return. A poltergeist 'infestation', as in some of the cases described previously, can involve many hundreds of individual incidents of extraordinary activity, while in other cases there are only a handful of curious and inexplicable happenings. Some 'hauntings' comprise single solitary events that are clearly unexplainable, but are real to their percipients nonetheless. Such is the case with the following story, which took place in Stevenage during the mid-1960s.

Shortly before his marriage in 1964, long-time Stevenage resident Richard Mott of Meadow Way, Bedwell, was living in a room at Sishes Mansion, a large Victorian-era house converted into a youth centre. The building was located off Meredith Road on the outskirts of Sishes Wood and at that time there were a number of teenagers living in the house. One evening a group of residents were sitting around an open fire in one of the large downstairs rooms. The house had very high ceilings and there was a tall bay with large sash windows. As the group sat talking the large curtain which was drawn across the bay suddenly opened by itself as though being parted by invisible hands. The curtains remained open for a few seconds before falling back into place and all the people in the room witnessed the curious happening. Describing the incident to the present writer, Richard remains adamant that the movement of the curtain had not been caused by a draft coming through the sash windows (the obvious explanation) or air movement created by someone opening a door. It was just as though someone had parted the curtain to look out (or more sinisterly to look *into* the room) and then closed them again.

Elsewhere in this book we have seen how the presence of lively young and particularly adolescent people seems to provide some kind of stimulus for psychical activity to take place. This is particularly the case where poltergeist phenomena are concerned. Was this some kind of telekinetic phenomenon created by the collective 'energies' of the teenagers in the room, relaxed and enjoying each other's company? Or was Sishes Mansion itself a haunted building and had one of its ghostly occupants decided to make its presence felt? Richard Mott himself had no further experiences and shortly afterwards moved out of the house. The building was subsequently demolished in the late 1960/early 1970s and a small estate of houses comprising Sutcliffe Close now occupies the site. Whether there are any further accounts of ghostly activity at Sishes Mansion waiting to be rediscovered remains to be seen.

Stepping Back in Time

Timeslips, the creation of what amount to temporary displacements or 'windows' that seemingly give access to both past and future times, have become a reasonably familiar concept in the public mind

thanks to television programmes such as the long-running *Doctor Who*, the dinosaur-infested *Primeval* and (for those that can remember it) Irwin Allen's *The Time Tunnel*. The world of ghosts and hauntings contains many examples of these alleged occurrences that are more common than would at first be expected, while a number are regarded as controversial classics. The most famous of these, the Versailles case, has divided the opinions of researchers since details were first published over one hundred years ago. On a hot summer day in August 1901, two former principals of St Hugh's College, Oxford, Miss Moberly and Miss Jourdain, were visiting the gardens of the Petit Trianon when they seemingly slipped back in time and found themselves walking through the grounds as they would have been during the reign of Louis XIV. The two women claimed to have seen buildings and garden features that were no longer in existence and encountered solid-looking apparitions of courtiers in authentic period clothing as well as the ghost of Marie Antoinette herself. Another notable case, this time a wholly audible timeslip, took place again in France, this time in 1951, when two English sisters-in-law heard what has been claimed to have been a ghostly re-enactment of the disastrous Allied raid on the German-occupied coastal town of Dieppe on 19 August 1942. The women reported the sounds of gunfire, dive-bombers, explosions and the cries of wounded soldiers, which corresponded with the actual times the real fighting took place nine years previously.

Other timeslips are less well known but equally as baffling. In *The Mask of Time* (1978), Joan Forman, author of a number of paranormal-related books, describes the experience of a small 7-year-old boy from Hanley, Staffordshire, who, while playing truant from school in 1896, walked through a doorway in a wall at the end of a cul-de-sac and found himself in 'a different world, a small town with houses nothing like I had ever seen before'. Beyond the town the landscape sloped down into a valley and beyond it were low tree-covered hills. Eleven years later, the same boy, now a soldier assigned to the 4th Army Headquarters, entered a village called Misery in northern France and realised he was in the place of his earlier 'vision'. 'The landscape was exactly as I had found it before.' Even more bizarre was the discovery made, decades later when he visited his childhood home in the early 1960s: in his boyhood timeslip he saw the street through the archway named 'Windmill Street'; now the area had since been redeveloped and one new estate road was (and still is) called Windmill Street.

There is an account of what appears to have been a timeslip-type incident which took place in the centre of Stevenage New Town during the early 1980s. Lisa West's (pseudonym) mother Mary (pseudonym) moved to Stevenage from London in the mid-1950s. In an interview in 2014, Lisa recalled how she heard her mother recount an extraordinary experience after returning home from a routine shopping trip. As Mary had walked out of the rear exit of the Marks & Spencer store she was confronted by an inexplicable sight. Instead of the Marshgate car park with St George's Way beyond, the scene she was greeted with was *completely different*, as though she was then suddenly part of a landscape from 'several hundred years' before. There were no cars, lamp posts, high-rise concrete buildings or tarmac. Instead, Lisa West's mother described seeing an almost rural scene. What buildings were visible were small

The Marshgate car park, where a strange timeslip experience took place in the early 1980s. (Paul Adams)

dwellings, farmhouse-like, and scattered amongst areas of open land. There was a rudimentary road, more in the nature of a farmer's track. Like the people in the Versailles vision that appeared to Miss Moberly and Miss Jourdain, the people who were also visible were dressed in costumes from a completely different time period.

According to Mary West, the entire vision lasted for approximately a minute before it blurred and was suddenly gone as though returning into the mists of time. Instead of the ghostly landscape of former times there was ordinary modern reality. The experience was never repeated. Mary West came out of the same exit into Marshgate on several other occasions but never again did she have what appears to have been a brief look back at an area of rural Stevenage from former times. This kind of phenomenon is more common than would at first be thought. My friend Ed Brazil, who has co-authored three paranormal books with me and has written the foreword to the present title, has described to me a similar experience involving his own father, who one day in the 1960s opened the bedroom curtains in his room in their house in Camberwell, South London, and saw, instead of the street and urban buildings, a wide landscape of trees and open countryside. Like that of Mary West in Stevenage, the vision lasted a minute or so and then faded away, never to be repeated. I have no explanation for such experiences. It is possible that some could be created by a powerful hallucination, but how to explain such incidents as recorded by Joan Forman, where the timeslip seemed to provide a premonition of future times? Such is the mystery and fascination of the paranormal world.

The Woman in Black

Many people experience psychical phenomena at a young age and those experiences stay with them for many years afterwards. We have already encountered the experiences of Chris Body whose susceptibility to psychic phenomena made him vulnerable to the attentions of the Stevenage Poltergeist. Cases of children and the young seeing ghosts can prove to be highly convincing. Many children enjoy creating imaginary playmates, but it would seem highly likely that a proportion of these childhood friends are apparitions or psychic visions that only they can see and interact with – see my *Haunted Luton & Dunstable* (p.35) for an eerie case of a ghost child named Beatrice who appeared to step out of the wall at bath time!

An often-reported happening with both children and adults is that of waking and seeing an apparition standing silently at the foot of the bed. Sometimes it is recognised as a family member who has died or in many cases is an unknown person who may or may not attempt to communicate in some way. Some of these ghostly encounters can be explained away by natural causes. When falling asleep or waking we can all experience what are known as hypnagogic and hypnopompic states which were first described by a Dutch physician way back in the middle of the seventeenth century. These are sensory hallucinations often involving vivid sounds and visual experiences that can be misinterpreted as paranormal or ghostly manifestations. As a child I can recall several hypnagogic experiences when on the edge of falling asleep which involved encountering an unnerving dark presence which appeared to come menacingly towards me across a bizarre surreal plain like something out of the old 1982 science-fiction film, *Tron*.

Although it is possible to explain away many individual ghost sightings in this way, there are numerous reports of people seeing ghosts in their bedrooms during the night that cannot be so easily dismissed. The Paddocks is a long residential road to the south of the Six Hills Way and it was here that another lifelong Stevenage resident, Amanda Stelling, had a number of strange experiences as a child. Over several years, beginning when she was 3 to 4 years old, Amanda was aware of the figure of a tall woman dressed in black who would appear at night upstairs in the house, an ordinary local authority-built dwelling with no prior history of unusual happenings. Remembering the incidents today, she describes the woman as being aged between 30 and 40, and who she sensed was looking for her own children who had been killed in a fire many years before in the Bedwell district of the town.

As well as Amanda herself, the apparition, always dressed in black and never speaking, was seen by other people, mainly babysitters who would encounter the figure on opening the bedroom door periodically to check on the sleeping children inside, as well as Amanda's brother, eighteen months younger than her, who also slept in the same room and saw the ghost himself. These encounters proved to be too much and a number of babysitters refused to go back to the house.

Interestingly, the house in The Paddocks appears to have been a case of multiple-haunting, something often encountered in the history of paranormal investigation. Here Amanda and others were aware of a male presence which manifested in the hallway and created the sound of marching footsteps up and down the stairs. Although the sound of footsteps were heard on many occasions, this particular ghost did not reveal itself and nothing was seen. After some time, a religious exorcism was carried out in the house (part of which was filmed by BBC television) after which Amanda and her family moved to another address. The house, which is still tenanted, appears to be quiet today.

Ghosts in the Family

Many paranormal groups taking part in organised vigils of haunted places carry out some form of séance as part of their investigation procedure. This can take various forms, either with or without a dedicated psychic or medium. Some researchers use a planchette, a crude writing instrument dating back to the heyday of Victorian Spiritualism, which allows words or scripts to be written down on sheets of paper; others employ the more familiar Ouija board as a means of trying to encourage communication with alleged spirits and 'entities'. Even people who have no real long-term interest in the paranormal have most likely experimented, often for their own amusement, with a Ouija-like device at some point, even in its most basic form of an upturned glass located inside a circle of letters drawn out on slips of paper.

Opinions are divided as to whether this is a good or bad idea. A recent supernatural horror film, *Ouija* (2014) directed by Stiles White, involving a group of American teenagers who release a demonic presence after trying to get in touch with a dead friend, presents a popular interpretation of using such a device. Other investigators claim that useful information can be obtained if certain procedures or protocols are employed to protect those taking part and to 'close down' the board safely at the end of the sitting to prevent anything nasty or potentially malignant from being left behind. This leads to the idea of whether it is possible in certain situations or environments to create a haunting by either encouraging the attention of spirits or providing suitable conditions in which they are able to manifest. We have seen how some people appear to unconsciously attract the attention of ghosts and apparitions simply by being the people that they are. Perhaps houses or buildings can act in a similar way through the activities, both good and bad, that have gone on in them in the past?

I became interested in this idea after speaking with Margaret and Mick Hughes and learning about some of the things that have gone on in the past in their home, an ordinary mid-terrace house on the south-eastern outskirts of Stevenage New Town. The couple have lived here for the past twenty-five years, during which time a number of strange and seemingly inexplicable incidents and happenings have taken place. Perhaps these have some of their origins in the activities of a former tenant, Pat Carrere (pseudonym), who lived in the house for some time before and had somewhat unusual and decidedly macabre views on the idea of internal home improvements. These in the main involved building a fireplace together with an internal partition to divide the large ground floor through lounge into two separate rooms

using salvaged gravestones. The actual origins of the stones are now obscure although Carrere claimed that they were given to him as a 'job lot' that he felt obliged to put to good use. This, combined with Ouija board parties held in the house in the past for kicks by groups of Carrere's friends may well have created some foundation for later events which soon began to take place after Margaret and Mick and their young family moved in.

During their time living in the house, all members of the Hughes family have both seen, felt and heard ghostly phenomena. A tall dark figure, insubstantial with no clearly discernible face or features, has been seen by Margaret herself in the hallway and also by several visitors to the house. There have also been dragging sounds (which, along with footsteps, are a common audible manifestation in haunted dwellings) as well as banging and rapping together with knocking noises heard and felt coming from a table. Much of this phenomena, including the movement and interference of objects, took place during a twelve-month period beginning in 1993 when Margaret and Mick's son was then aged 16. A tall house plant was seen shaking by itself under circumstances that ruled out draughts coming in through an open window or being disturbed by the house cats; while their son observed a pair of his own jeans being pulled along the end of the bed as he lay watching. On several occasions the zip fasteners on his friend's school bag were pulled open as they walked up the path toward the front door.

These incidents appear to be in the mould of poltergeist-type phenomena, thankfully much less destructive and distressing than that encountered in Byron

Close, and Margaret Hughes herself told me that she felt this aspect of the haunting was created by the sheer presence of young people growing up, accompanied by spontaneous outbursts of laughter and happiness. Although unnerving at times, there was no real sense of menace or threat. However, some of the happenings described to me have a decidedly darker side to them and seem to hint that perhaps at times the house and its family have been the focus of unwelcome and more disturbing forces.

On one occasion, Holly, a friend of Margaret's son, brought a tape recorder into the house with the intention of trying to record some of the ghostly activity. Ghost hunters often try to capture paranormal phenomena on tape and today EVP or Electronic Voice Phenomena is almost a standalone subject within paranormal research. Sceptics argue that the Electronic Voice Phenomena are simply created by a combination of ordinary static and the ability of the human brain to create seemingly intelligible words out of random sounds, with the result that, like 'orbs' and similar visual anomalies on photographs and video recordings, EVPs remain a controversial part of modern paranormal investigation. Most EVPs take the form of individual words or short staccato sentences which are audible on analogue or digital tape recorders, either appearing spontaneously or in response to specific questions posed by team members during the course of an investigation. The first person to encourage the serious study of EVPs was the Swedish psychologist Konstantin Raudive (1909–1974), whose pioneering book *Breakthrough* was published in an English translation (by Peter Bander who also wrote on the subject) in 1971. At Stevenage, Margaret

described hearing what appeared to be a male voice that was heard responding to specific questions on the tape. When Holly made the statement, 'I wouldn't want to see a ghost', a distinct reply of *'Why?'* was clearly heard. This was followed by a much more sinister exchange. To the question, 'How many spirits are in here?', the same gruff male voice replied, *'Count'*.

I have visited the Hughes' home several times. It has a unique atmosphere but not a frightening or disturbing one and things have been relatively quiet now for some time. It seems likely that here the phenomena reported was a combination of several factors. Both Margaret and Mick Hughes are undoubtedly psychic or have latent psychic abilities; there is also the presence of adolescent teenage children, an important factor where poltergeist-like phenomena is concerned, plus the strange behaviour and activities of the former tenant whose actions may well have created an atmosphere that encouraged certain phenomena to take place.

Night Visitors in Bedwell and Shephall

During a visit to the Red Lion in the Old Town while researching for this book, I met and spoke with Peter Burton (pseudonym) who, like Amanda Stelling in the previous case, has had experience of being visited by apparitions during the night hours. Burton described seeing the solid and lifelike figure of his own grandmother who appeared on two occasions ten years apart, the first in 1970 and again in 1980, in a house in Gonville Crescent in Shephall. She had fallen and broken her leg in three places in the late 1960s, never fully recovering from the

A phantom monk allegedly materialises in a haunted house. Many people claim to have seen similar apparitions in places with no actual connection with religious buildings or orders. (Author's collection)

shock and trauma of the incident and died shortly afterwards. The apparition, which had all the density and consistency of a living person, stood silently at the foot of the bed for a short time before vanishing. Each time Burton felt quite calm and accepted the incidents for what they were – a brief and treasured return from a much-loved family member.

Interestingly, Peter Burton's encounters with the paranormal appear to be separated by the passing of a decade of time, almost in the manner of a cyclical haunting. In early 1990 Burton was living in a house in Langthorne Avenue in Bedwell. One night, not long after retiring, he was lying in bed when he saw what he later described to me as a monk-like figure, complete with a hood covering the head

and face, which seemed to step out of the shadows in the corner of the room. As he watched, the figure moved around the bottom of the bed towards the bedroom door through which it seemed to pass and disappear. The figure made no sound during the time it was visible and appeared to be completely unaware of the observer's presence. Peter Burton was adamant that he had not dreamt either this experience or the earlier appearance of his grandmother in an entirely different house and location.

This latter experience begs the question: what is the apparition of a monk doing haunting a 1950s-built local authority house on a former greenfield site with no history of previous buildings or monastic or religious houses in the area? Rather than being the ghost or spirit of an actual medieval monk or friar it seems most likely that what Peter Burton saw that night was one of the curious manifestations associated with the appearance of apparitions. Many people describe ghostly figures as looking 'monk'-like in appearance in that they appear to be dressed in some form of robed attire, often accompanied by a hood or cowl covering the face. These figures are often associated with and encountered inside modern buildings. It would appear that whatever causes the hallucination of us witnessing or experiencing an apparition can at times only create what our brains subsequently translate as being that of a monk or religious figure, in the same way that many ghosts appear to be faceless or have their features concealed or hidden in some way. These are some of the similarities that can be observed in a broad range of paranormal encounters involving disparate locations and witnesses.

Strange Happenings in Aston Village

The Domesday village of Aston lies on the south-eastern outskirts of Stevenage on a rise above the valley of the River Beane. Despite its closeness to the New Town, the area retains its rural quality and there are many attractive period buildings, including the thirteenth-century church of St Mary's. Close by is the former site of Aston House, now demolished, used by the Special Operations Executive (SOE) for the development of explosives and sabotage weapons during the Second World War.

Des Turner has lived in Aston since the mid-1960s and has spent much time recording for posterity not only the history of the village but also Aston House

itself. In his book *Station 12: Aston House* (2006), Turner makes mention of the experiences of an SOE officer who spent time alone inside the rambling building while the secret weapons establishment was being set up. On several occasions a piano in one of the large downstairs rooms was heard to play by itself. On investigation, the room – together with the rest of the ground floor of the building – was found to be closed and locked. The demolition of the building – during the 1960s, around the time that Des Turner moved into the village – makes this one of Aston's intriguing and now lost hauntings.

As well as its orthodox history, the psychic fabric of Aston also contains some interesting and unusual happenings. Several people have described to me the strange atmosphere at a particular spot along the footpath that leads from the footbridge over Aston End Brook and Gresley Way to the north end of Dene Lane. This would appear to be some form of psychic residue of an event in the past – most likely unpleasant – which lingers and is picked up by suitably aware people walking along this particular route. To the south of the village at Astonbury Wood, which lies to the immediate north of the A602 road, Ruth Stratton and Nicholas Connell have collected an account of a haunting associated with the apparition of a knight dressed in armour who is said to have been seen riding through the trees. Accounts are sketchy at best and the haunting appears to be little more than a colourful tale, probably encouraged by the discovery (in 1957) of a sixteenth-century sword in the wood by two local farmers.

As we have seen elsewhere in this book, people who encounter the paranormal at a young age often continue

Aston House (now demolished), where the sound of a piano playing by itself was heard during the Second World War. (Des Turner Collection)

to have psychic or ghostly experiences in later life. Such is the case with Mick Hughes whose home lies half a mile west of the centre of Aston village. As a young 15-year-old school leaver in the mid-1960s, Mick literally came face to face with a haunting apparition while working as a builder's labourer at a doctor's house in Hampton Court in Surrey. During the time that the contractors were refurbishing the building, several people, including Hughes himself, had the unnerving experience of seeing a tall black figure, substantial but with no discernible features, which made its presence felt on a number of occasions, passing by open doorways or appearing suddenly beside tradesmen as they carried on with their work. Among a number of unusual happenings which have occurred to Mick Hughes over the ensuing years, some of which will be related later on in this chapter, are two incidents which occurred in Aston village itself and show that as well as occurring when it is least expected, ghostly phenomena can take many baffling and unusual forms.

One night, Hughes was returning home following an evening out, his route taking him along Benington Road which runs into Broadwater Lane on the western side of the village. As he came level with St Mary's church, he became aware of a glowing ball of intensely white light, roughly the size of a cricket ball, which appeared out of the trees on the opposite side of the road, approximately 30ft off of the ground. Coming to a halt, Hughes watched as the orb-like light moved soundlessly and at an even pace across the road, passed over the lych gate at the entrance to the churchyard and disappeared from sight behind the tower of the church. In total the strange light, which immediately brings to mind the natural phenomenon of ball lightning, was visible for approximately thirty seconds. However, ball lightning is associated with atmospheric disturbances and thunderstorms, and on this occasion the night was clear and bright with no hint of rain or storm.

Following the mass application of digital filming and photography over the past fifteen years, the term 'orb' has entered, with much subsequent controversy, into the language and literature of paranormal investigation. Anomalies present on video films and digital photographs have been championed by some psychics and researchers as evidence for the appearance of ghosts and spirit forms, and although it remains an interesting idea, today most researchers are confident that this 'orb' phenomena is in fact created by unseen dust particles and moisture vapour that is picked up by the digital media in a way that is not possible with traditional film and still photography. It seems highly likely that what Mick Hughes saw outside St Mary's church that night was what American ghost hunters call a 'spook light' and in Britain is known more traditionally as a 'will-o'-wisp'. These atmospheric ghost lights are reported from many cultures around the world although they are most commonly described in America and Japan. A famous American case is the Joplin Spook Light which has been reported for many years near the town of Hornet on the border between north-eastern Oklahoma and south-western Missouri. What actually causes these strange lights to appear is unclear and they have been variously interpreted as wandering spirits of the dead and, in more recent times, manifestations of UFO phenomena.

There are a number of listed buildings of historic interest across Aston village of which the Rose and Crown pub in Benington Road, a short walk from St Mary's church, is one. Built originally as a private house in the sixteenth century, part of the building dates from this period while the remaining sections, added a hundred years or so later, were heavily renovated by a brewery

Broadwater Lane in Aston village opposite St Mary's church, where Mick Hughes saw a 'spook light' drift over the road one night. (Paul Adams)

The Rose & Crown pub in Aston village, haunted by a ghostly cat and the apparition of a young girl. (Paul Adams)

company in the early 1950s. There is a tradition that the large garden to the rear of the pub (currently closed at the time of writing – February 2015) is haunted by the figure of a young girl wearing an old-fashioned dress who is thought to be lost and searching for her family. Perhaps there is some connection with this apparition and the ghostly atmosphere sensed in nearby Dene Lane.

In the Rose & Crown itself something akin to a ghostly cat has been experienced at least once and collectively by several people at the same time. One warm summer day, Mick Hughes, together with a group of three other people including the then landlady, Lorraine Thorne, were sitting at a table at the front of the pub next to an open window facing the roadway. During a lull in the conversation, Lorraine and Mick became aware of what he describes as a moving patch of luminous mist which appeared like a flash at the open window and then dropped down out of sight between the table and the wall. Almost immediately there was the impression of something brushing past his leg under the table which was also experienced by one of the group, a man named Steve, who became unnerved by the incident. The whole experience was as if a cat had jumped up from the pavement outside through the open window and made its way across the room between the sitters' legs. Was it one of several cats which were known to live in the pub in the past? Although tame by the standards of some of the paranormal encounters included in the present book, it remains a curious incident which was felt by at least two people at the same time.

The Ghost of Lady's Wood

While carrying out research for this book I was fortunate to meet Des Turner, the Aston village historian mentioned previously in connection with his chronicling of the secret war work at Aston House. Des has kindly allowed me to reproduce an article originally written for a Christmas number of the *Aston Parish Magazine* which describes the sinister apparition known at one time by older villagers as the Ghost of Lady's Wood. The article is presented complete with Des' original introduction and epilogue, which hints at further ghostly happenings connected with this outwardly placid and tranquil location:

When I began collecting Aston's history [Des Turner writes], I advertised in the Hertfordshire Countryside *magazine, inviting people to contact me if they had any information about this village. I received a letter from Mr Eric F. Kingsley of Baldock, aged 67, who wrote: 'I have a story that I must tell you.' I drove to his home on 10th September 1970, and was astonished to find a room full of family and friends who had gathered to hear this story one more time.*

He began: 'Back in September 1926 I worked as a gardener at the Dene for Mr Thomas Morton. I lodged in the village with Mr and Mrs George Brown, a very old couple, in cottages at Queen's Square (now demolished), standing next to the Rose and Crown. There was no main water supply, no electricity and no sewerage system. I lived in Baldock and cycled home every other weekend. One night, around midnight, cycling back to Aston, I rode up the steep hill on Broadwater Lane and reached the slight downward slope, heading towards Dene Lane. There were shadowy trees and hedges on either side, it wasn't what you'd call dark – there was a bright moon in a cloudy sky. I suppose it was mid-summer. I was freewheeling down the slope when I saw something dark in the road ahead of me. I thought it was horse droppings or something like that, but as I passed the object it appeared to be a cat. As I rode on I wondered if it had been run over, so I turned back to check that it was all right. I got off my push-bike, bent down, and sure enough it was a black cat and it was unhurt. I remounted and continued towards the church. At that moment I was surprised to see a middle-aged woman walking ahead of me in the same direction, at the side of the road. I thought, this is very late for a woman to be out on her own, when suddenly I was gripped by a strange force drawing me towards her, causing me to ride straight at her – it was powerful, magnetic and uncontrollable, I was on a direct collision course! I knew it was a crazy thing to happen and used the greatest strength I have ever conjured up in my whole life, to turn the handlebars and avoid riding into her. Right up to the very last split-second I expected an impact, when to my infinite relief, I missed her! I arrived at my lodgings in a confused state and went to bed.

Next morning, when I was at breakfast with my landlord, I said, "You've got some strange people walking about here late at night!" I told him that I had seen this woman and asked, "Could it have been Mrs Sturt, the Rectors wife?" He said, "No, it wasn't her, because they are away on holiday." "Well, what does Mrs Yeomans of Aston House, look like?" "Oh! she's a very old woman and doesn't go out."

I said, "Well, whoever it was, she's got a nerve walking about like that, on her own at that time of night!"

I arrived for work at the Dene and asked old George Church, a retired gardener from the lodge in Dene Lane, whom he thought this lady might be. He said, "I know who that was, you saw the Ghost of Lady's Wood!"

He went on: "It appears that many years ago a woman walking from Aston Bury to the church was murdered and her body was discovered in Lady's Wood. You saw her ghost." [The wood is now confined within the Stevenage Golf Centre, but there is a public footpath through its centre.] Well I didn't believe him, and just laughed it off. I decided it was one of those old village legends that you should never take too seriously, and dismissed it!

Subsequently, I passed that same spot dozens of times, it didn't worry me at all, and I thought no more about it. I left my job at the Dene in October 1929, returned home to Baldock and got married. My three years in Aston are among the happiest of my life. I met my wife there – she was in service at the Dene. We both got on very well with Mr and Mrs Morton and their two daughters and two sons, but alas, not with the head-gardener. He was the reason I decided to leave.

Two or three years passed and then one evening I was with a group of friends and we began to discuss ghost stories. I related my experience with the Ghost of Lady's Wood, how I felt compelled to run into her – and try as I might – could not steer my bicycle away from a direct collision course. One of the gentlemen present, a Mr Wilmot, said, "It's a good job you didn't run into her, for if you had, you would not be alive today! My father saw her when he was a gamekeeper. He was routinely checking his birds one night in Lady's Wood, and making sure there were no poachers about, when he spotted a woman and called out to her, but she didn't answer. He shouted louder, and was still ignored. He then moved closer and struck out at her with his stick and she just disappeared! He returned home in a state of shock and told his family what had happened. Next day he had a fit and died. If you had run into that woman you too would be dead!"

This astonishing revelation caused me to rethink the incident through and I realised there was a part of it that I could not explain. When I saw that cat I was going down the slope and continued almost to Dene Lane, not a great distance, but I would have passed that woman twice, and I only saw her once! When I went back to check that the cat was all right, the woman wasn't there! I also remembered that she didn't appear to walk but glided along without a sound. Was the cat with her? I wondered – it was sitting in exactly the same place when I returned to it. Could it have been transfixed by her vision? It makes me wonder if there really are such things as ghosts?

I had heard of this particular ghost from other sources. One person described it as a headless figure and I asked Eric if he could confirm or deny this? He remembered that she wore a long dress and he thought that her head was actually in place! Recently, two schoolboys reported seeing a ghostly figure of a woman by the Cynthia Wood footpath – 'You could see right through her!' Ken Clark, of Poplar Farm, Aston End, told me he once had a horse that would play up in Aston Lane and always had to be led past Lady's Wood. Personally, I have cycled by the wood several times after midnight, in the moonlight, and have quickened my pace whilst dwelling on these tales. A poltergeist was also brought to my attention in a house in Aston End Road. This was very alarming and frightening because objects were actually thrown across the room.

The Face at the Window

Shephall Manor lies to the south of the A602 Broadhall Way, equidistant between its junctions with Broadwater Crescent to the west and Oaks Close to the east. A large country house, it was designed by the English architect Thomas Roger Smith (1830–1903) who like others of his era were involved in constructing public works buildings for the British Raj in India. As well as his colonial architecture, Smith also worked on a number of private houses in England including Brambletye House in East Grinstead, West Sussex, and Hitcham Hall in Buckinghamshire. He was in his early thirties when he was given the commission by Unwin Heathcote for a new residence and Shephall Manor was eventually completed in 1865.

Unwin Heathcote died in 1893 and his descendants continued to live on at Shephall until the 1920s when the Heathcotes left and the extensive house was rented out to a series of tenants. In 1939, on the eve of war, Michael Heathcote sold the house and its estate to William Harriman Moss and over the next six years it was put to various uses as part of the war effort. Through the Waifs and Strays Society, the Moss family gave board and lodgings to thirty-two

Shephall Manor, photographed in the early 1900s during the time that the Heathcote family were in residence. (Richard Holton – www.shephallmanor.net)

Shephall Manor during the late 1980s when the ghost hunter Ashley Knibb saw a mysterious female figure at one of the windows. (Richard Holton – www.shephallmanor.net)

children between the ages of 2 and 5 evacuated from London, while towards the end of the war it served as a base for Polish officers. The manor's Polish connection was to continue for some time after the war. After being bought by the Stevenage Development Corporation in September 1947 it spent most of the 1950s as a school for Polish children. In 1960, the house was leased to the old London County Council which reopened the house as a boys' school and continued to run it as such until the late 1980s. Following a period of neglect in the early 1990s when the building and its grounds stood empty (during which time the manor became a Grade II listed building), it was ultimately bought by the Christian Coptic Orthodox Church in 1991 and it is as a cultural centre that Unwin Heathcote's former country house continues to be used today.

Stevenage resident Ashley Knibb, a long-time member of the Anglia Paranormal Investigation Society (APIS), has known Shephall Manor for many years and in fact credits experiences connected with the old house as being those that kindled his now lengthy interest in psychical research and the supernatural. One summer during the long school holiday period, Ashley, then aged around 11 years old, together with several friends, amused themselves by using the Shephall Manor estate as a playground. This was during the time (1990) that the Shephall Manor School had closed and the building had been left empty. On several occasions while playing in the deserted grounds, Ashley Knibb was aware of a woman wearing what appeared to be a dark-coloured dress who he observed standing and looking out of one of the numerous windows on the first floor of the house. Although it was possible that it could have been a caretaker or a cleaner (although the former school premises were clearly shut at this time and there were no cars or similar signs of visitors) something about the woman suggested that what he was seeing was not an ordinary living person. 'She was completely odd,' Ashley, remembering the incidents many years later, told me in an email in February 2015. 'She just stood there staring out across the garden. There were also a few times when the same woman was spotted in one of the more attic-style room windows, still staring out …'

On one occasion during this period, Ashley was able to get inside the house but never made it to the first floor to investigate if the face at the window was real or not. 'I can still recall the woman herself vividly,' he says. 'She had long curly hair, possibly brown or black and what appeared from my position a long dress. Interestingly she only remained as long as I gazed upon her – if I was distracted or looked away, when I look[ed] back she would be gone.' Perhaps significantly the sighting of the figure was not a collective one. 'As far as I am aware no one else shared this experience with me.' Who was the solitary lady looking out from this attractive and atmospheric building? Was it one of the Heathcote family, returning to the home she had known and enjoyed in life? If so, there may be occasions when this particular ghost can be seen again.

An Invisible Playmate

As has been noted earlier, dogs and cats are notoriously psychic creatures. There are many accounts of them behaving strangely in allegedly haunted buildings and reacting to what appear to be invisible presences and similar strange phenomena. The bond of love and friendship between animals (particularly dogs) and their owners seems on occasion to be able to survive beyond the grave: owners can sometimes get a feeling if an animal is sick or distressed and apparitions of pets are reported as appearing in favourite spots or locations around the house. Many dogs become terrified where psychic happenings are concerned, often reacting angrily or aggressively to forms that only they appear to be able to see. In St Nicholas' churchyard we have seen a dog that was ambivalent to the appearance of ghostly phenomena. An unusual account of a dog appearing to *enjoy* an encounter with an invisible playmate is given by Shirley Clancy who has lived in the Stevenage area all of her life.

One day in the mid-1960s, Shirley, then aged around 14 or 15 years old, was walking her dog along the eastern end of the Six Hills Way towards the junction with Chells Way. As she passed along the wooded section between the Ashtree and Great Collens Woods, the dog, which was walking off the lead, began behaving strangely. As Shirley watched, the animal began running around in a figure of eight shape and started jumping up and down as though someone was standing by the roadside and encouraging it to play. For Shirley, both she and the dog were completely alone, but she soon realised that the animal was interacting with something that only it could see, all the time happily wagging its tail and panting with excitement as it ran back and forth as though being thrown an invisible stick.

Unable to explain the incident, Shirley continued walking along the roadside in the direction of Chells Way but her pet, oblivious in its enjoyment, continued to run and jump about. Normally obedient, it refused to be encouraged to continue with the walk and eventually Shirley had to go back and physically pick the dog up and walk away with it under her arm. What the creature actually saw and experienced remains unknown from that day to this.

The Prudish Ghost of Sish Lane

Named after the fourteenth-century landowner John Sish (Shish or Shush), Sish Lane runs eastward from the southern end of the Old Town High Street to a junction with Grace Way. Sish was one of twelve surveyors appointed by the lord of the manor, the Abbot of Westminster, in 1315 to audit land and property in and around Stevenage in order to assess rents and other obligations that were due from the various tenants of the time. Before the development of the New Town, the road led into farmland and today, lined on both sides with post-war housing, it is difficult to imagine its former rural atmosphere.

The home of Karen Quinn is a typical early 1950s local authority house of the period. Karen and her family moved to Sish Lane over twenty years ago but from the start it was clear that despite its apparent normality, the property was a strange and at times unusual place. All members of the household were soon aware of an unnatural oppressive atmosphere which was centred on a dining room at the rear of the house. This feeling would come

and go, and was accompanied by sensations of coldness together with psychic 'touches', as though an unseen person was deliberately trying to make its presence felt. On regular occasions over the years, Karen has also been aware of what she describes as a tall dark figure which is glimpsed moving along the hallway from the kitchen towards the front door. Like many instances of regular apparition-like phenomena in haunted houses, this figure is seen out of the corner of the eye in the observer's peripheral vision and is instantly gone when one of the family is aware of its appearance. For a period when the dining room was used as a bedroom, all those who slept there complained about the intense coldness of the atmosphere – the room is adjacent to the party wall with the next-door house and part of the main building (with only one external wall) rather than being in an extension or back-addition which would be more likely to be naturally colder than the main house.

What is unusual in the case of this haunted house in Sish Lane is that the phenomena associated with the dining room remained dormant until the subject of sex would come up in the general conversation (!), after which incidents of the nature described above would start to happen and continue for several days before dying down again. A number of researchers have in the past explored the connections between sex and the supernatural, for instance in its relationship with poltergeist activity and mediumistic phenomena but here, as Karen notes, it is almost as if the ghost has a prudish attitude to the subject. The previous occupier had lived in the house since it was built and died a fortnight after Karen Quinn and her family had moved in. Many houses appear to contain some aspect of the presence of former owners and occupiers and in this case it seems that perhaps whatever may return to the house in Sish Lane from time to time considers some subjects not to be suitable for general conversation at meal times!

The Ghosts of Little Wymondley Priory

From the various accounts included in this chapter it is clear that paranormal or psychical activity can take place as easily in a modern dwelling or council house as in an ancient castle, ruin or sumptuous stately home. We have also seen that ordinary people from all walks of life see apparitions and encounter ghostly activity in the most mundane of places and, importantly, when they are least expecting it. For the final entry in the present book we leave Stevenage's twentieth-century post-war suburbs and visit what is very much a traditional location where one would expect ghosts to linger on down through the passing years.

The village of Little Wymondley lies 2½ miles north-west of Stevenage. It was here around 1216 that an Augustinian priory was founded by Richard de Argentein whose family eventually held the honour of being cupbearers at the King's Coronation for over 600 years, the last being at the coronation feast of George IV on 19 July 1821. Richard took part in the Crusades on two occasions, the first in Egypt in 1218 where he was involved in the assault on Damietta, and again in 1240, defending the Citadel of Jerusalem before its final fall to the invading Turks. The de Argentein family

also were responsible for the upkeep of the fourteenth-century parish church of St Mary's at Little Wymondley while Richard himself died in 1246 after what for those times was a relatively long and successful career.

The Augustinians, initially founded at the request of Henry I at Colchester in 1105, were a religious order who lived the dual role of monks and local preachers. At one time there were in the region of 200 houses at various locations across England, including Cirencester, Bristol, Osney and Walsingham, but by the time of the Dissolution of the Monasteries by Henry VIII around 1538, only thirty-two remained. The monks, whose scalps were unshaved, wore long black cassocks with a white vestment or rochet, over which was a black cloak and hood. The priory at Little Wymondley comprised a church together with a refectory, chapter house, dormitory, kitchens and outbuildings which were grouped around a central courtyard space or cloister. Following the Dissolution, the priory was given as a private house to the Nedeham family originally from Derbyshire. Records mention James Nedeham, an architect and carpenter who in 1525 served as a gunner in the Tower of London, as well as his son John who inherited the priory from his father. In 1688, George Nedeham took on the priory and began to make improvements and alterations.

Up until the beginning of the eighteenth century much of the priory, including the cloister, was extant but today only part of the original unaisled church nave survives, the remaining sections of the building, together with the outer priory complex, having vanished over the years. There is a surviving Tudor

The priory at Little Wymondley, now a private house, allegedly haunted by the apparition of a former prior. (Paul Adams)

wing, although eastern parts of the building as a whole are thought to have been destroyed in a fire in the eighteenth century. In 1973, the priory was stripped to a shell and refurbished into a modern residence. In 1991, John Hope and his family bought the house together with its grounds and the adjacent sixteenth-century tithe barn, originally constructed by James Nedeham, which is used today as a wedding venue.

Historic hauntings associated with Little Wymondley Priory were collected by William Gerish for his *A Tour Through Hertfordshire* which was originally published in 1921. Gerish lists two supernatural occurrences which are straight out of the standard haunted house tradition, namely the appearance of a phantom monk, in this instance the apparition of a former prior, said to have been seen wandering in the roadway on the approach to the priory, together with an indelible bloodstain which was recorded on a flagstone in the priory crypt or cellar. There is little or no modern evidence for either of these manifestations. John Hope, discussing the subjects of ghosts at Little Wymondley with the present author, has not seen or heard reports of the ghostly prior during his ownership of the priory, while the bloodstain, if it did exist in the past, would have been lost to sight during the 1970s when the cellars or basement areas of the surviving building were infilled as part of the extensive refurbishment work.

However, it does seem that on occasion, strange things are reported by visitors to Little Wymondley Priory. In 1997, a female house guest of the Hope family, who was staying in one of the second-floor bedrooms located directly over the former nave of the old priory, woke her hosts in the middle of the night in a considerable state of distress. A short time before, she herself had been roused from her sleep by the disturbing sight of the wardrobe and cupboard doors in the bedroom opening and slamming closed by themselves. At the same time she also had the unpleasant sensation as if some invisible person was tilting the bed itself and attempting to try and throw her off on to the floor. Another curious incident is connected with the historic aisled tithe barn, built of oak in nine bays measuring a total of 102ft long by 39ft wide, making it one of the largest of its kind in the country. Shortly after the Hopes had moved to Wymondley, Nike Mohan, an architect employed to carry out restoration work on the property, visited the barn to carry out a survey of the structure. During the course of his inspection he took numerous photographs of the exterior and interior of the tithe barn. On one of these shots of the interior looking up into the roof area, a curious swirl of white smoky substance is clearly visible close to the camera lens and partially obscuring the timberwork behind. Photographs taken immediately before and after the 'ghost' picture on the same roll of film were completely normal. Mohan's photograph is an interesting one and is very similar to a number of images captured during investigations of allegedly haunted buildings

Little Wymondley Priory – the historic tithe barn. (Paul Adams)

and locations. According to the way it is viewed, the smoky shape has been interpreted as that of the figure of a knight or a figure on horseback, although interpretations of this kind are very subjective. What is interesting is both the spontaneous nature of the phenomenon and the fact that the other photographs taken at the time show no such anomaly, proving that it was not a camera or film fault. The photograph is reproduced below so see what you think.

In 2001 the Ghost Club Society, a private paranormal club with a long interest in psychical matters and ghost hunting, held an all-night vigil inside the tithe barn. The visit was somewhat uneventful, although at one point the batteries on several cameras including a video camera all suddenly became drained of power,

A curious smoke-like anomaly, photographed by architect Nike Mohan in the tithe barn at Little Wymondley Priory in the early 1990s. (John Hope)

despite being fully charged prior to the beginning of the investigation. This curious phenomenon has been reported by many paranormal investigators in numerous locations across the country and is generally assumed to be some manifestation of localised psychical activity.

One aspect of Little Wymondley Priory which is of interest to paranormalists is its geographical position, being located on the famous St Michael's ley-line. The St Michael's ley-line starts at St Michael's Mount in Cornwall and extends north-west following the path of the sun on 8 May (the Spring festival of St Michael) across the southern half of England, picking up a number of ancient sites along the way including The Hurlers stone circles (also in Cornwall), Glastonbury Tor, Silbury Hill in Wiltshire (the largest man-made prehistoric structure in Europe) and the Waulad's Bank henge at Marsh Farm, Luton. At Stevenage it passes through Little Wymondley Priory before continuing on to Bury St Edmunds Abbey and ending at Hopton-on-Sea on the Norfolk coast. The term ley-line was first adopted by an amateur archaeologist, Alfred Watkins, who developed his theories in a book, *The Old Straight Track*, published in 1925. Leys represent the geographical alignment of natural features in the landscape, primarily ancient sites such as burial mounds, barrows, stone circles and tumuli. Watkins felt that these ley-lines were simply ancient pathways that were used by our primitive forebears as trade routes between locations across the country. However, a Wiltshire solicitor and Justice of the Peace, Guy Underwood, realised that these lines could be detected by dowsing and as such formed natural pathways along which a natural energy or 'earth force' could flow from place to place. These energies were, according to Underwood, known to priests and adepts of the old pagan or pre-Christian religions, which was why they built their ancient temples and places of worship (like the stone formation of Stonehenge) on the lines themselves or at points where several ley-lines intersect. Some paranormal researchers now suggest that leys can act as conduits or channels for psychical activity and, as such, buildings or locations which fall under the lines are more likely to be haunted or display instances of ghostly or psychical activity. The presence of old stone walls and similar timbers and brickwork at Little Wymondley Priory would also suggest that perhaps the idea of the 'stone tape' theory of haunting mentioned earlier may also be relevant here.

This brings us to the end of our survey of ghosts and hauntings in and around the Old and New Town of Stevenage. Clearly the twilight and mysterious realm of the paranormal is continually interacting with our own, wherever we are. Outside there is mundane normality: rush-hour traffic, grey skies, noisy conversation, a mobile phone ringing; while inside, without warning, strange things outside of normality are taking place: a

Alfred Watkins (1855–1935), an amateur archaeologist who coined the term 'ley-line' for the alignment of ancient sites and formations across the country. (Author's collection)

door opens on its own, footsteps sound in an empty corridor, a light comes on by itself, a toy is twitched off a shelf as if by an unseen hand, while something moves in a glimpse out of the corner of the eye, perhaps even now as you glance up after reading this final page …

FURTHER READING AND RESEARCH

Select Bibliography

Adams, Paul and Brazil, Eddie, *Extreme Hauntings* (The History Press, Stroud, 2013)

Ashby, Margaret, *Stevenage: History & Guide* (Tempus Publishing, Stroud, 2002)

Broughall, Tony and Adams, Paul, *Two Haunted Counties* (The Limbury Press, Luton, 2010)

Burton, Jean, *Heyday of a Wizard: Daniel Home the Medium* (Harrap, London, 1948)

Farrant, David, *Dark Journey* (British Psychic & Occult Society, London, 2004)

Forman, Joan, *The Mask of Time* (MacDonald and Jane's, London, 1978)

Gerish, W.B., *Tour Through Hertfordshire* (C.H. Peacock, Watford, 1921)

Hine, Reginald L., *Confessions of an Un-Common Attorney* (J.M. Dent & Sons Ltd, London, 1945)

O'Dell, Damien, *Ghostly Hertfordshire: True Ghost Stories* (Pen Press Publishers Ltd, Islington, 2005)

Playfair, Guy Lyon, *This House is Haunted: The Investigation of the Enfield Poltergeist* (Souvenir Press, London, 1980)

Price, Harry, *Poltergeist Over England* (Country Life Ltd, London, 1945)

Puttick, Betty, *Ghosts of Hertfordshire* (Countryside Books, Newbury, 1994)

Rogo, D. Scott, *The Haunted House Handbook* (Tempo Books, New York, 1978)

Stratton, Ruth and Connell, Nicholas, *Haunted Hertfordshire: A Ghostly Gazetteer* (Book Castle Publishing, Copt Hewick, 2010)

Turner, Des, *Station 12: Aston House – SOE's Secret Centre* (The History Press, Stroud, 2006)

Underwood, Peter, *No Common Task: The Autobiography of a Ghost-hunter* (Harrap, London, 1983)

Ward, Mrs E.M., *Memories of Ninety Years* (Hutchinson, London, 1924)

Local Paranormal Groups

A Hertfordshire-based ghost-hunting organisation with an interest in Stevenage hauntings is Damien O'Dell's Anglia Paranormal Investigation Society (APIS). APIS is always keen to involve serious-minded people with an interest in the paranormal in their investigations. Details can be found on their website: www.apisteamspirit.co.uk.

Based in neighbouring Bedfordshire, the Luton Paranormal Society (LPS) is a well-established investigative group with a yearly programme of visits to haunted locations throughout the three counties of Hertfordshire, Bedfordshire and Buckinghamshire. There is an extensive database of local hauntings including several Stevenage cases on the society's website: www.lutonparanormal.com.

National Paranormal Organisations

For anyone involved in serious research into the paranormal, membership of the following three British societies should be considered. They are the Ghost Club (www.ghostclub.org.uk), founded in 1862; ASSAP, the Association for the Scientific Study of Anomalous Phenomena (www.assap.ac.uk), founded in 1981; and the SPR, the Society for Psychical Research (www.spr.ac.uk), established in 1882. Their publications and archives contain invaluable information and resource material, much of which is now being made available online.

Some Paranormal Websites

The following Internet sites contain useful information on ghosts, hauntings and similar supernormal phenomena:

www.davidfarrant.org
David Farrant – Psychic Investigator – Known for his involvement in the Highgate Vampire affair of the late 1960s/ early 1970s and founder of the long-standing British Psychic and Occult Society, David Farrant (*b*.1946) has carried out personal investigations of many haunted buildings and locations around Britain, details of which, as well as information on his many books and video documentaries, are available on this website.

www.ghostresearch.org
Ghost Research Society – The GRS, originally known as The Ghost Trackers Club, was founded in 1977 to collect real life reports of ghosts, poltergeists, hauntings and survival after death experiences across America. The Society president is Dale Kaczmarek (*b*.1952), one of America's most experienced ghost hunters.

www.harrypricewebsite.co.uk
The Harry Price Website – An online collection of articles on the career of Britain's famous ghost hunter, including a comprehensive section on the Borley Rectory case.

www.mysteriousbritain.co.uk
Mysterious Britain & Ireland – A comprehensive resource of information on the hauntings, legends, folklore and mysterious places of the British Isles.

www.paranormaldatabase.com
The Paranormal Database – A comprehensive and continually updated online gazetteer of ghosts and hauntings across England, Scotland, Ireland, Wales and the Channel Islands.

www.prairieghosts.com
American Hauntings – Website of author and ghost hunter Troy Taylor (*b*.1966), founder of the American Ghost Society, which contains links to The Haunted Museum online resource on the history of paranormal and psychical research.

ABOUT THE AUTHOR

PAUL ADAMS was born in Epsom, Surrey, in 1966. Brought up on a diet of Hammer films and British pulp-horror literature, a major preoccupation with the paranormal began in the mid-1970s with a visit to the much-haunted Sandford Orcas Manor House near Sherborne in Dorset. Employed as a draughtsman in the UK construction industry for over thirty years before becoming a full-time writer

Paul Adams at Snagov Monastery in Romania in 2014, researching the legend of Vlad the Impaler for a book on vampires and vampirism. (David Saunderson)

in 2014, he has worked in three haunted buildings but has yet to see a true ghost. As well as the history of psychical research, his interests also include materialisation mediumship and the physical phenomena of Spiritualism. He has contributed articles to a number of paranormal magazines and acted as editor and publisher for *Two Haunted Counties* (2010), the memoirs of Luton ghost hunter, Tony Broughall. Adams is the co-author of *The Borley Rectory Companion* (2009), *Shadows in the Nave* (2011) and *Extreme Hauntings: Britain's Most Terrifying Ghosts* (2013), and has written *Haunted Luton and Dunstable* (2012), *Haunted St Albans* (2013), *Ghosts & Gallows* (2012), *The Little Book of Ghosts* (2014) and *Written in Blood* (2014), a history of vampires and vampirism in British culture, all for The History Press. He is also an amateur mycologist and viola player and has lived in Luton since 2006.

Website: www.pauladamsauthor.co.uk
Twitter: @PaulAdamsAuthor

Lightning Source UK Ltd.
Milton Keynes UK
UKOW06f1215010915

257877UK00001B/16/P